DISCOVERIES

DISCOVERIES

EXPANDING YOUR CHILD'S VOCATIONAL HORIZONS

RICHARD P. OLSON
HELEN E. FROYD

UNITED CHURCH PRESS
CLEVELAND, OHIO

United Church Press, Cleveland, Ohio 44115
© 1995 by Richard P. Olson and Helen E. Froyd

Printed in the United States of America on acid-free paper

Library of Congress Cataloging-in-Publication Data

Olson, Richard P.
   Discoveries : expanding your child's vocational horizons / Richard P. Olson and Helen E. Froyd.
        p.   cm.
   Includes bibliographical references (p.   ) and index.
   ISBN 0-8298-1106-0 (alk. paper)
   1. Vocational guidance. 2. Parent and child. 3. Career education. I. Froyd, Helen E. (Helen Elizabeth), 1935–   . II. Title.
HF5381.058   1995
331.7'02—dc20   95-16997
                                           CIP

CONTENTS

PREFACE

Helen Froyd, at various times in her life, has worked as an employ-ment adviser for developmentally disabled young adults, as a staff member for a private career counseling agency, and as a caregiver for older adults.

Richard Olson is a clergyman who has counseled many youths and young adults through various decisions about life directions. Dick has done research on vocational decisions of persons sixteen to twenty years old and has written a book on that subject. He has offered life-/ career-planning workshops for middle-high persons, high school per-sons, college persons, and postcollege persons of all ages. In these workshops, he attempts to integrate a view of Christian vocation with helpful exercises from such career counselors as Richard Bolles.

It was while Dick was conducting such a workshop for middle-aged adults at Helen's home church that we first met. Our mutual interests stirred a friendship and a desire to learn more from each other. One evening after the close of a session, Helen asked, "Do you know of any books that help parents offer this sort of vocational discovery to their children?" Dick didn't, but his curiosity was stimulated. We both searched and found a few resources but nothing that included all that we felt important. And so we resolved to put such a book together.

We read widely— various types of psychology, family-life literature, writings on Christian vocation, futuristics, and anything that held possi-ble application. We interviewed a number of career counselors, pastors, and theologians about how they applied their knowledge to their own parenting tasks. We asked questions of many people, young and old.

Thanks are due to the many people who shared a thought or re-source, who read and evaluated a chapter or more, and who encouraged this project.

Here are the results of our search. This book is written for a wide range of parents and caregivers—from those with newborn babies to those whose children are young adults. Not everything in this book will interest every parent or caregiver. Here, then, is our suggested road map through this book:

- Begin by reading chapters 1, 2, and 3.

- Then select a chapter from 4 to 7 that matches the age of your oldest child.

- Next, turn to chapter 8.

- From there, go to whatever holds interest. You may want to consider the other age groups. You may be interested in the chapters that provide the supporting information (9–11).

One more word of self-introduction. Helen is the parent of two adult children, and she is a grandparent. Dick has three adult children and four grandchildren. We know both the difficulty and the importance of the subjects of this book. Our fond hope is that we will lend a little aid and encouragement to that company of parents of which we are a part.

P A R T

1

FAMILIES AND VOCATION: AN OVERVIEW

The word vocation comes from the Latin *vocare*, to call, and means the work [one] is called to do by God.

There are all different kinds of voices calling you to all different kinds of work, and the problem is to find out which is the voice of God. . . .

By and large a good rule for finding out is this. The kind of work God usually calls you to is the kind of work (a) that you need most to do and (b) that the world most needs to have done. . . .

The place God calls you to is the place where your deep gladness and the world's deep hunger meet.[1]

—Frederick Buechner

The work of which Buechner speaks is more than employment. It includes relationships, leisure, and learning—all a person does or is.

When one fully grasps this concept of vocation, communicating it becomes one of the most important parenting tasks. Vocational leadership of children is a specific Christian responsibility. It also represents the goal, the result of Christian parenting. However, the task of parental vocational leadership has had little attention. It is a responsibility that may make many parents uneasy.

And so we begin our conversation by looking at resistances to this parental role, at basic ways a parent can address this task, and at the Christian vision that informs us.

Possible Road Map for Reading Part 1. Quite possibly, you will want to read these three chapters in order. However, if you want to know the faith perspective that informs all else that we say, read chapter 3 first and then read the others.

The Gift You May Not Know You Have

Every child comes into the world with the message that God is not yet discouraged with the world—for God has continued to create this special person." These words from a service for consecration of children express a central truth: A child is promise—a special, unique creation of God. Parents and all who love a child gather around and wonder, "What will this child be?"

Out of this fascination with each child's potential we are led to an important discovery. We propose that parents have a vital gift to offer their children. That gift is a continuing contribution to the child's occupational discoveries. If indeed a child is promise, the Christian concept of vocation suggests that the child has a place in God's will. Vocational discovery, exploration of that place to which God calls one, is a lifelong process. Its development begins earlier and continues later than most people realize. Parents are with their children from infancy through young adulthood. Therefore, parents are the right people to offer vocational guidance to their children as they try to sort out which of the more than forty-five thousand occupations available in today's world they would like to pursue.

We well realize that much of what we suggest is not new. Parents have undertaken this task in every generation. However, it is a subject neglected in many books on parenting. As we (Helen and Dick) look back, we notice that there was more we could have done with our own children. Perhaps you are feeling the same way. If so, explore this process of being parental vocational guides for your children.

At this point you may well be resisting our suggestion, raising one or more of the objections we address in the sections that follow.

OBJECTION 1

"I don't know enough about what's most appropriate for them."

Don't you, really? Does anyone know your children better than you do? If anyone does, recruit that person's help as well! However, parents know much about their children and what might be the most fitting for them.

We are not suggesting that parents should take over making vocational choices for their children. Each person's decision must be his or her own. However, parents do indeed know enough to help children discover some good possible directions in which to begin their career search.

OBJECTION 2

"There's somebody else who can do this much better for my children than I."

And who might that person be? their schoolteacher? the guidance counselor at the school? some professional vocational counselor? adult friends of your children? same-aged friends? a clergy member or youth leader at your church? All these individuals could well be resources in helping your child make significant discoveries. Still, the one who will have to integrate all this guidance will be the child. We suspect that you as parent are the ablest guide and most available person to help your child integrate that information.

OBJECTION 3

"I'm so proud of my children that I have no objectivity about them. Someone who can more accurately measure them against others should help them with their vocational decisions."

A sturdy and solid self-esteem is an excellent place to start in choosing a vocation! It is wholesome for a child to believe "I am a good person, and I have some valuable gifts/talents." Such a child has a good start on effective career decisions. We doubt that you will hinder your children by letting them know that each of them is special and unique. Your awareness of each child's gifts may powerfully influence his or her self-discovery.

Of course there are times when your perception of your child's talents will be measured against other children's giftedness. This will be especially true in competitive fields. Although parental pride can be occasionally overdone, your belief in your child can be one of your significant contributions in his or her vocational discovery.

OBJECTION 4

"Won't I damage them if I hold too high a goal before them?"

Yes. It can be destructive to force on children goals higher than they are capable of reaching or than they wish to reach. Your question reflects a healthy caution that many well-intentioned parents need to have. There is a delicate balance between holding a child accountable to do his or her best and pushing the child too hard.

There is yet another aspect to this. Some parents *unintentionally* force excessively high goals upon their children simply by being high-achieving adults themselves. This can make the children afraid to compete—sometimes choosing to avoid their parent's occupational area and sometimes feeling they cannot measure up to their parents in any field.

When parents suspect that they are in some way forcing too-high expectations upon their children, they will want to explore this. Perhaps open conversation about what the child is experiencing can remove some of the hidden pressure. Caring parents will attempt to reduce the barriers that stand in the way of their children making wise and free decisions.

OBJECTION 5

"I'm too rushed to do what you say. All the time I have to offer my children is taken. I feed them, clothe them, earn enough income to provide for them, and drive them to their various activities. Other people have my children much more than I do. My influence with them is very small."

We identify with this reservation! One of us is a single parent, the other a parent in a two-career family. The pressure of time is real. Very few of us invest as much time and energy in parenting as we would like to.

However, what we propose is not necessarily a much larger time investment in parenting. We are suggesting, instead, a consciousness, an awareness, a way of understanding one of the goals of parenting. In the little time parents have, they can plan activities purposefully. They also can help their children integrate their thoughts and experiences in an effective way.

The keys are awareness and conversation. What do you talk about when you are with your children? In the time you have, you can make conscious use of opportunities for talking about interests, skills, and activities that develop the child's self-image and self-direction.

OBJECTION 6

"My children reject my methods, my values, my work style. They're not interested in what I have to share with them about vocational choice."

Youth is a time of sorting out. It is also a time for becoming different and claiming one's own identity. And so parents may expect some questioning and criticizing of their lifestyles. (In chapter 6, we will explore this in more detail.) However, parents and children still may have things to learn from one other as they work on vocational decisions together.

If you feel strong enough to hear the answer, ask your child, "To what in my lifestyle, my values, do you object? How do you want to be different? What steps can we take to help you become the way you want to be?"

You might also want to take time to communicate what your values are and why you choose the work styles that you do. The choices your son or daughter will one day make will not be as clear-cut as they now appear to him or her as a teenager. That teenager is entitled to this search. However, you can be a part of it.

OBJECTION 7

"It's a different world out there. My offspring are more at home in it than I am. Let them lead me!"

I (Dick) well understand that feeling! One of my daughters once gave me a simple video game. I have never been able to manage it, while my children and grandchildren do quite well at it. Each member of my family knows a good bit more about computer operation and management than I do. This information seems to be very much a part of the future of every occupation, including mine.

In considering the technologies of the present and future, a parent may feel inept and inadequate. Certainly, it is easy to feel helpless when considering being a vocational guide to children who are going into such a world. Any parent who has tried to help a child with math discovers concepts and methods that were not taught a generation ago! Many persons coaching youngsters in sports have discovered that children may now outperform us quite early.

It would be a shame to let our awareness of what we do not know crowd our awareness of what we do know. We have much to offer: knowledge and wisdom gained by the experience of living; awareness of our children's strengths and weaknesses; firsthand experience of opportunities in the world of work; global and social awareness; our own faith perspective; and assessment of family resources available to aid our children in their search and preparation.

It can be an enriching experience to let our children teach us their newly discovered computer skills and other new knowledge. Then we can inquire about their dreams of what they want to do with such skills.

OBJECTION 8

"My children are teenagers (or young adults), and they are completely out of my control or even influence. I don't approve of many of their choices, but they still make them. They and I have nothing to say to each other about vocational decisions."

Indeed, these young adults are working on a most important aspect of themselves—a sense of autonomy, independence, and self-direction. This will quite likely be an uncomfortable time both for them and for the parents and other adults who care about them. They may now reject adult input that they would have at least considered at an earlier age. (See chapter 7 for further thoughts on this issue.) However, this does not mean that parents are fired as persons involved in the vocation

process—at least not completely fired. It does mean that the parent's role has changed. Probably the parents are no longer directors of the child's vocational discoveries (and they probably never were!). They are now simply consultants. Like good consultants, they know they can offer what information they have to share when asked. They also know the information may be accepted or rejected. Still, the patient parent can know that this process is necessary for the child to achieve independence. The young adult's independence is a shared goal.

Although we are speaking of youthful behavior that shows a desire for independence, young people rarely can be completely independent. They probably still have some dependence on parents in a financial sense. This might be a place where the dialogue can begin. For example, discussions might address how much money they will need to earn to be independent, what preparation they will need to earn the necessary money, what that preparation will cost, and how that cost will be managed. We will return to some findings on this topic as well.

OBJECTION 9

"Children and young people these days don't believe in planning. Some are worried about war and an unstable world. Others fear that no matter what, they face unemployment. They may not think there is an endurable future to plan for."

Fortunately, this fear is decreasing. It has not, however, entirely gone away. This is a solemn concern that must command the attention of us all. However, it is most disturbing to those who have most of their lives and careers before them, if the world survives.

The parent who senses that such fears are paralyzing a child's planning has an important barrier to address. A first step might be to find some way to talk out the fear. Another way might be to help the child enter into activities that impact the nuclear arms race. One of my (Dick's) friends lives near a nuclear weapons plant. Her children are quite aware that it would be a first target in event of attack, and they often spoke of how they would be annihilated if this should happen. Then the opportunity came to participate in a demonstration, in which several thousand people would ring the area of the plant. My friend's children wanted to participate, and so their parents took them. They noted that the children did not talk about their fears as much after that. The plant is still there, and so in one sense the protest was ineffective. Yet the children sensed that they could be a part of influencing the system. Apparently, they don't feel as paralyzed by fear as they once did.

Consider also that this fear presents some significant vocational questions, such as: If I'm concerned about the threat of nuclear war, what do I want to do about it? How can I contribute to the world's peace and justice? If the world endures, what part would I like to have in it?

If your son or daughter's fear is of unemployment, read on. (Especially see chapter 11, where we speak of employment trends and predictions.) You may be able to help your child find the opportunities that hold great promise of employment in the future.

Objection 10

"I don't feel I have anything to offer my children because I'm not very happy with my own job these days."

Welcome to the club! We recently heard the estimate that 85 percent of all people have some job frustration. There are many reasons for this lack of job satisfaction on a day-to-day basis. We must spend so much of our time there—even when we would like to be doing something more interesting. Routine and boredom creep into familiar tasks. Deadlines and seasonal demands take their toll. Many of us have been at the same occupations for many years and are no longer excited about them. So much competition exists for the really creative jobs that many people feel their skills are not adequately used.

When we feel such work frustrations (meanwhile attempting to guide our children), we may need to ask ourselves some questions. One question might be, "How frustrated am I?" If the frustration is relatively mild, parents can recognize and communicate to their family the good parts of the job: the things they believe in about the work, the camaraderie of co-workers, the benefits, the pay. However, if this frustration is deeper, perhaps they need to ask, "What is it that I *truly* want; how can I get there? What training, what risks, will I need to take to enter into something more meaningful to me?" Parents might be surprised by the family support they will receive in dealing with such frustrations.

In asking these questions, parents may be offering their children a very special gift—an example of thinking, planning, and acting to achieve a more satisfying future. This process also gives children an example of an important contemporary truth—that often persons can change jobs or careers when it is fitting to do so.

OBJECTION 11

"I don't feel informed or confident about the spiritual dimension of vocation that was mentioned earlier in this chapter."

In chapter 3, we will offer help in claiming one's beliefs about Christian vocation and applying them to one's own life and one's children's lives. Whether or not parents are aware of their own views on Christian vocation, these views are implicit in good parenting. For example, Evelyn and James Whitehead offer this definition, "A Christian vocation is . . . an invitation to make something good and holy of our lives."[1] Our awareness that when entrusted with a child we have been allowed to share God's continuing creation, our sense of wonder about the miracle of life, and our fond hopes for the child's greatest possible opportunities are all spiritual aspects of Christian vocation. If we convey that much to our children, we are well on the way to communicating Christian calling.

You may not have thought about this or thought you had little to offer. Think again! Feel free to question, but stick with us as we attempt to wear down your resistance. We will begin with a few simple suggestions. Then we will develop these ideas in a variety of ways. We hope to show you not only *why* but *how* you can share with your children the gift you may not know you have—the gift of vocational wisdom.

2

What the Caring Parent Can Offer:
A Preview

We begin by suggesting a simple list of things caring parents can do to aid their children's vocational discovery. Before we do, however, let's think a moment about terms. Often the words "occupation," "career," and "vocation" are used interchangeably. We have a distinction in mind: "occupation" describes employment; "career" includes the series of jobs a person has in the course of a lifetime; "vocation" refers not only to employment but to all aspects of a person—work plus hobbies, relationships, volunteer activities, and more. In chapter 3, we will explore the more profound understanding of vocation as "calling"—from God.

This chapter is a brief preview. We will add details for each age group in chapters 4 through 7. Then, we will enrich these suggestions and offer others, with a number of examples, in chapter 8. To open our exploration together, we will begin by suggesting nine things a caring parent can do.

1. Encourage Your Child's Education

Wherever we turned in our explorations, we were struck with the fact that the educational qualifications and demands will be higher for tomorrow's worker. Your enthusiasm for your child's schooling is important. Take time to look at the child's papers. Let the child read to you. Some experts suggest that having a child read aloud for fifteen minutes a day has dramatic effects on reading and educational skill. Attend school events and parent-teacher conferences. Make it a point to know the answer to this question: Is your child gaining the foundation necessary for future learning?

We think of a young man who dropped out of high school and who spoke wistfully of missing his class's high school graduation. The problem, he said, was that as he fell further and further behind his classmates, he became more and more uncomfortable. Finally, the discomfort was so great that he dropped out. When asked the last time that he felt comfortable in school, he answered, "second grade."

His story haunts us. We wish for him and for every child parents who are proactive in encouraging a good fit and mastery of needed skills at every level of schooling.

2. Support "Normal Development" in Your Child

We will discuss developmental tasks for each age group in the chapters that follow. We offer this information with the awareness that there are tremendous variations among children who are all normal. The ages at which children walk, talk, learn to count or read vary widely. For the most part, that is entirely okay and has little or no bearing on your child's future. If you are concerned, a talk with a teacher, school counselor, or doctor may well set your mind at ease.

At this point, however, we speak of something else. There are two parental traps to avoid. One trap is pushing the child too hard. We agree with those who write with alarm about the "hurried child." Pushing the child to learn ahead of his or her time, to dress older, date sooner, grow up faster is not a good idea, from our point of view. (We are not resisting any learning or discovering a child does, responding in joy and curiosity to stimulation provided by parents.)

The other trap is holding the child back. Some parents enjoy the child so much that they cling. When the time comes for the child to go to half-day school, full-day school, summer camp, or college, the parent has a hard time letting go. This in turn makes separation more difficult for the child. Going forward together—mutual letting go—is much more encouraging.

3. ACCEPT YOUR CHILD AS SHE OR HE IS

In personality style, interests, and gifts, a child will not be the carbon copy of either parent. Nor will the child be half of one and half of the other. The child may have quite different strengths from the parents, and quite different weaknesses. If you have more than one child, each will quite likely be different from another in these qualities. This is not failure—it is life!

Parents need the loving wisdom to accept each child as an individual and be confident that there is a good career destination for him or her. This includes the unexpected child, who should never be made to feel like "an accident."

Some children grow up worrying that there is something wrong with them. This is particularly true of the introvert personality type, who especially at an early age, may be somewhat shy and withdrawn. Fortunate is such a child who has a parent who understands and accepts him or her as a unique individual.

Parents sometimes communicate nonacceptance in another way as well. Adults may have had a great experience that they want the child to repeat. (I was a good basketball player and made the team. I want you to do the same thing.) Or, they may have had a frustrating experience that they want the child to correct. (I was not a good basketball player and didn't make the team. I want you to go out and make the team for both of us.) It is not fair to ask a child to live out your dreams—children are entitled to their own dreams. Of course, it's fun if, after all those games on the driveway, the child loves basketball as you do. Happily, some interests and dreams are shared. Whatever way it goes, children need to know they are accepted as the individuals that they are.

4. ENCOURAGE YOUR CHILD'S SENSE OF SELF-WORTH

If you can help your children feel good about themselves, you have given a valuable gift. The child will be able to face unknown situations, make decisions, and take advantage of suitable opportunities.

You can do this by the attention and the sincere praise you bestow on the child. You can also do this by the special time you spend individually with a child. Employed parents may often need to squeeze such times into meals or when driving from one event to the next. You can note things that the child does well that he or she may not recognize. You can be supportive when the child gets disappointing feedback from teachers, schoolmates, or siblings.

There will be times when you are angry or upset with your son or daughter. There will also be times that you will need to discipline him or her. These occasions may be crucial for the child's sense of self-worth. Even at those times (especially at those times!), do not do or say anything to destroy the child's self-image. While you may need to disapprove of a given behavior, do not label your child with words such as "dumb, stupid, lazy, awkward, selfish, mean," or, especially, "sissy" or "tomboyish."

In all the stress and strain of daily family living, attempt constantly to tell your child, "I accept you; I believe in you; I trust you enough to hold you accountable! I am confident about who you are and who you will become."

5. RECOGNIZE AND DEAL WITH PITFALLS

There are so many things that can get in the way of a good healthy life of learning, developing self-esteem, and vocational discovery. As a parent, be aware of potential pitfalls. Avoid them if possible, and deal with them if they arise in your child's or family's life.

One of these potential pitfalls may be TV and other mass media—or rather, indiscriminate overuse of media. Studies are indicating that too much television can contribute to passivity and thereby lower achievement in school. TV also can become a substitute for interaction and thus hinder development of "people skills."

Another potential pitfall is anything that prevents school from being a good experience. Transfers, illness, a hostile or tense environment, fear, violence, a difference between school philosophy and a child's learning style—these factors and others can interrupt a good learning experience.

Still other potential pitfalls include employment that demands too many hours during school, involvement with alcohol or other drugs, sexual difficulties, a teenage pregnancy.

When you encounter such pitfalls with your child, do not see them as the end. Rather they are obstacles for which the family will need the shared ingenuity to overcome. Every human being will make some mistakes, and every person will have some failures. Children who learn to face these, overcome them, and correct their course have done something very important. Not only have they have faced one problem, they have also gained strength to deal with issues that will undoubtedly arise in the future.

6. Model, Teach, and Expect Good Habits of Work and Play

Albert Schweitzer once noted, "There are only three ways to teach a child: the first is by example, the second is by example, the third is by example."[1]

Whether you know it or not, as an adult you have a style of work. This style includes many things: your commitment and energy for the work you do; your integrity, reliability, enthusiasm, and enjoyment; your punctuality, attention to detail, and the way you respond to pressure. You express this working style both at your place of employment and at home when you do the tasks needed for maintaining a household and family.

You also have a style of play. You have a preferred response to many issues around play: Can you play before the work is done? Can you play in the midst of work? When you both want to work and to play, which do you choose? What is play for you?

Your children may imitate or reject your style of work and play. One thing they cannot do is ignore it! It will be a strong influence in their lives, one way or the other.

You will be wise to maintain a lifestyle of work and play that makes sense to you. When given opportunity, interpret it. There may be parts of it that you cannot explain, such as why you are so driven at times. Be honest about those factors as well.

A child who grows up knowing how to work effectively and play with abandon has received a wondrous gift!

7. Expand Your Child's Experiences

A child's imagination and curiosity are wonderful. Given free reign (limited only by concerns for safety), a youngster may eagerly discover an ever-growing world. The child will find numerous things to touch, taste, look at, or hold. He or she may be filled with even more questions. While you as parent may lack the time and energy to respond to all these explorations and questions, do not suppress a child's curiosity. It is a valuable tool, and it seems to diminish all too quickly in some persons.

Your child's eventual choice of a career will be limited by the world he or she has experienced. Therefore, it is important for your child to have had an adequate range of experience to make a wise choice.

So, in addition to your child's curiosity and imagination, add another valuable resource—your own. Sometimes you may be aware of things to investigate that your child is not. Explore them together. Near and far, look for new things for your child and you to discover and experience together.

There is a simple but important technique in career development called the "field survey." This consists of talking to people who do something as a hobby or occupation that interests you and asking them the following four questions: "How did you get into this?" "What do you like most about it?" "What do you like least about it?" and "Who else can tell me more about it?"

Parents and children together can learn to do children's versions of "field surveys." If, for example, your child loves the outdoors, it will be wise not only to go to parks, zoos, and lakes but to visit with park rangers, gardeners, commercial fishers, farmers, and zoo employees. In a few moments of conversation, see what they do, experience their world. Your child's world will have grown, and his or her range of choices will have expanded.

As the child grows older, longer visits, volunteer service, and short-term employment can broaden the fund of information and range of choices. Creative children and parents will discover innumerable ways to expand experiences and choices.

8. Encourage Independence and Decision-Making Skills

In child-rearing, a parent needs to maintain simultaneously two perspectives: (a) I am fully with you now, in this moment; and (b) you and I need to be ready for you to leave. Those two points of view are difficult to reconcile, but both are necessary and important.

As a parent enjoys a child, the parent should take every opportunity to help the child develop skills for independent living and deciding. When the child grows older, he or she can learn basic survival skills: fixing a simple meal; doing laundry; doing yard work; caring for a car, including checking oil and changing a tire; making local and long-distance phone calls; writing a thank-you note, etc.

We are aware of a family with two school-aged daughters. This family has developed a unique addition to children's birthday celebrations. With each birthday, the girl is given a new chore or responsibility to mark her growing abilities. Those parents are wise indeed—developing responsibility is an important gift.

Whenever there is a choice between doing something *for* the child or doing it *with* the child, choose the latter. Rather than open a bank account for the child, take him or her with you to do it together. Learning to perform tasks such as operating an automatic teller machine, making deposits, and inquiring about a job provides opportunities to develop independent-living skills.

An area of independent living that needs special attention is that of making decisions. Little by little, teach your child to think through decisions. Discuss the positives, the negatives, the possible outcomes. Then let the child decide. Important learning comes from living with the consequences one's own decisions.

Decision making can be taught with money. Providing an allowance and giving the child latitude in deciding how to spend it may be a first step in decision making. I (Dick) used the following technique with my children. After experiencing vacations in which there were hassles at every souvenir stand about what the children could or could not have, I tried something different. At the outset of a trip, I would tell my children, "You may each have X dollars' worth of souvenirs. You may have all or part of that money at any time you wish. But, when that money is spent, it is spent." This not only provided a valuable lesson for the children but less stress for me.

Decision making will also occur as the child moves into later school years and chooses some of his or her own courses. A wise parent will want to be aware of and discuss these decisions. The parental message to a child is something like this: "We hope you will make these decisions so that you will have the widest possible range of choices in the future. Let's talk about where these decisions lead. More and more, decisions about your future will be yours. We want to be close and available to help with each of those decisions, if you need us." With this style, parent and child will be more ready for those decisions about post–high school plans that will come in the junior and senior years.

9. SPEAK AND LIVE YOUR FAITH AND VALUES

In Deuteronomy 6, believing parents are reminded that God is one and that we are to love God with all our heart, soul, and might. Then parents are given explicit instructions: "you shall teach [God's words] diligently to your children, and shall talk of them when you sit in your house, and when you walk by the way, and when you lie down, and when you rise. . . . And you shall write them on the doorposts of your house and on your gates" (Deut. 6:7, 9).

In other words, let your beliefs and convictions become so much a part of you that you spontaneously express them in every rhythm of living. Look for opportunities to speak of faith and opportunities to live out faith. Don't save such communications with your children for big, formal occasions. Let them be a part of life.

Of course, formal religious practices are also important. Prayers at meals and with children, specific times of reading together Bible stories and other literature of faith, observance of religious holidays—these too are part of communicating that faith that includes your vocational vision.

Parents need not wait until their faith feels "complete" to share these beliefs and hopes. It will always be in process. Furthermore, if you grow or maybe even change your mind and communicate that to your children, you have set an important example. They will feel more free to grow, develop, change in their faith as well.

We feel that a vital part of sharing faith and vocational vision is to find a church and to participate faithfully. People in a group help one another to communicate their faith and provide a variety of role models for all of their children. Faith and vision are mutually strengthened.

Your children deserve to know where you stand. If you tell them honestly, you don't need to worry about overwhelming them. They will one day make perfectly clear to you that they are capable of choosing their own life's direction. That is as it must be.

These are some of the ways parents can contribute to their children's career and vocational discovery. Shortly, we will look for these opportunities at each stage of a child's life. Before we do, we will look at the core faith that informs us.

3

Christian Perspectives on the Vocational Quest

The happiest people in the world are those who have found the life task to which they have been called. And the most unhappy are those who have not even begun the search.[1]

The vocational quest involves discovering one's interests and skills as well as employment opportunities where these characteristics fit. However, there is another, deeper dimension to this search. This additional dimension appears in such questions as "Where am I most needed? What occupation will be most meaningful? Where can I do the most good? What is my calling? What does God want me to do with my life?"

Unless these questions are answered satisfactorily, one may experience discontent with one's work, regardless of how well it fits in other ways. These are questions of values. They speak of a basic hunger for meaning and reveal a desire to be in harmony with the universe and with the source of the universe.

Our Christian faith says a good deal to us about our hunger for meaning and direction. This faith offers perspectives for the decisions and management of our lives. Let us reflect on what our faith offers us in this regard. We will first describe for you what this says to us as adults. Then we will explore implications of this faith vision for parenting. Finally, we will come back to the broad-based questions and reflections with which we started this chapter.

20

CHRISTIAN VOCATION FOR ADULTS

The basic perspective in our faith is the concept of Christian vocation. The term "vocation" is not used as precisely these days as we might wish. When persons speak of vocation, they might be talking about their occupation or about a particular family of occupations, as in "vocational school." However, this term has its root in the Latin word *voco,* which means "call." (The word "vocal" has the same root.) And so, to speak of one's vocation is to speak of one's call—from God!

This is a familiar concept in both Hebrew and Christian scriptures. The Bible is literally full of God's calls. God calls the children of Israel into a covenanted relationship. God calls the church into being. God calls individuals to specific responsibilities within those covenant groups. Jesus calls persons to be his disciples, engaging in lifelong service, witness, and learning. God's call to us as a community and as individuals is a frequent, basic teaching of the Bible.

The apostle Paul gave a new dimension to this general understanding. He offered an important insight, almost as an aside in a consideration of other matters. Paul was discussing issues of Christian decision in an uncertain pagan society. At one point he said, "Let every [one] abide in the same *calling* wherein [one] was *called*" (1 Cor. 7:20, KJV) [emphasis mine]. Note that he used the term "call" twice in the same sentence. The second time he mentioned "call" in that sentence, he referred to one's calling to be a follower of God. The first usage of "call" referred to one's circumstance in life. He speaks of three circumstances: the first has to do with marital status; the second with whether or not one is circumcised (and thereby one's family, religious, and cultural heritage); the third with whether one is slave or free (and therefore one's economic status and occupation). In essence, Paul said to his readers, "Recognize that your present circumstances and responsibilities are part of your call from God. Your situation in life comprises at least one aspect of your vocation!"

To summarize, the Bible offers the teaching of Christian vocation—that is of God's call to each and to all. When this is a basic presupposition, important discoveries emerge. Let's explore some of these insights.

1. Everyone Has a Call

First, each person has a call, not just those persons in church-related occupations. Whiteheads put it well:

> Every Christian is called. And we are called over a lifetime. A Christian vocation is not a "specialty"; it refers not only to the priesthood or vowed religious life, but to the particular direction and purpose that every maturing believer is expected to find and follow.[2]

God has called all of us into covenants (agreements, promises, and relationships with God). When we believe that, then all questions about ourselves and our identities become questions about our vocations as well.

James Fowler notes that we move from the question "Who am I" to *"Whose* am I?" After we gain an idea of who we are as seen through the eyes of those around us, we come to an even more basic question, "Who am I in relation to the Creator, Ruler, and Redeemer-Liberator of the universe?" As he notes, when one comes to this perspective, every question of identity becomes a question of vocation.[3]

Walter Brueggemann suggests that vocation is "a purpose for being in the world that is related to the purposes of God."[4] Vocation seen in this way is the opportunity of every person.

Elton Trueblood, who has long been concerned with this subject, points out how relevant religious faith becomes when it helps people discover the hidden glory of the common things they do. This vision is needed—the principle of vocation—to "lift our sagging civilization." He concludes, "We come to believe that the world is one, secular and sacred. Therefore, an important way to serve the Lord is in our daily work."[5]

2. Vocation Is More than One's Occupation

Second, while one's vocation includes one's occupation or career, it is not identical with one's occupation. It includes much more than that. This view of vocation also includes persons who may not be able to have an occupation due to illness, infirmity, or age. James Fowler suggests, *"Vocation is the response a person makes with his or her total self to the address of God and to the call to partnership.*" The discovering of one's unique vocation involves the orchestration of many aspects of one's being. These include our leisure, our relationships, our work, our private life, our public life, and the resources we manage. As Fowler notes, the term "orchestration" is carefully chosen. It implies the artistry of combining one's unique opportunities, gifts, and challenges in the same way that various instruments of orchestra blend together.[6]

Perhaps the idea of vocation as the response of a person's total self will be made clearer with an example. Carlyle Marney offers us such a memory from his childhood. For thirteen years, his family enjoyed the wondrous four gallons of thick creamy milk that their Blue Jersey cow "Daisy" gave them. This incredible supply of good milk, day after day, provided for the Marney family and for other nearby families as well. Yet each year there was a crisis. Each time Daisy bore a calf, she suffered terribly from mastitis. Marney recalls the agony:

> Groaning with pain from her swollen udders, the new milk locked in bulging mammaries, she would sink in her stall floor to die of fever on the very lip of a season 's flood of lovely milk. Except—except for Mr. Adams' vocation.
>
> President of our small town bank, he lived just across the alley in a wide, low house. Four A.M.; new calf in the stall; Daisy down on her knees; Mr. Adams with his bicycle pump and ointments and hot water under Daisy's big belly; my father with Daisy's tail over his shoulder straining to keep her hindquarters from going down. While an amateur veterinarian, bank president, Presbyterian elder, neighbor, father pumped and oiled and soothed Daisy into production for another season.
>
> This is vocation!

After telling his story, Marney goes on to reflect: "But who is Mr. Adams? Was he neighbor, elder on a Christian mission, banker serving a very modest customer, or a cattle-loving veterinarian with a sympathy for a hurting beast whose name came from the side of a churn? Answer: He was all of these at once."

Carlyle Marney concludes, "The term for the whole—role, work, proper end—is *vocation.*"[7]

3. Vocation Is What One Is at One's Core

It is also fitting to speak of vocation as what a person is at that person's very core. A person's central identity, greatest passion, most basic conviction, most fundamental commitment is one's vocation. Bruce Larson makes this clear by fantasizing a conversation with the apostle Paul:

If you asked Paul, "Who are you?" what do you suppose he would say? He could answer,

> "I am a tentmaker. I am a very efficient, competent, creative tentmaker. My bids are competitive. . . . I think I am one of the best in the business. I spent forty or fifty hours a week making tents." He could say that, but he probably would not, even though that might be a quite accurate answer. More likely he would say something like this: "Let me tell you, God has given me a calling to bring the Good News of Jesus Christ to the world. Incidentally, I make tents and spend a good part of my day doing that."[8]

As with the apostle Paul, each of us has opportunity to explore what our most central convictions are. Each of us is free to ask about the nature of our understanding of life's most central meaning. That, too, is our vocation.

4. Vocation Is What We Are

This brings us to a fourth discovery about vocation. It has to do not only with what we *do,* but also with what we *are.* There is a bit of children's verse that expresses this very well:

> *We have the nicest garbage man.*
> *He empties out our garbage can.*
> *My mother doesn't like his smell.*
> *But then, she doesn't know him well.*

Children see what others miss—their friends' vocations are not only the essential work they do but also the kind of people they are.

5. Our Relationships

A fifth discovery parallels the fourth. Vocation has to do with our relationships—how we cultivate them and what we do with them. We recall a man who drove the same bus route for years. He came to know the regular customers along that route so well that he greeted them by name. He learned about their joys and sorrows and made them feel welcome and valued on his bus. This driver created a jovial, friendly atmosphere for customers at the beginning and end of their work days. When he was rewarded for competent service by being promoted to dispatcher, his former riders felt a real loss. Other drivers may be kind and competent, but they never quite attained his loving, outgoing spirit.

We recall another fine example, a worker on the snow removal and park maintenance force for a large city. A recovering drug addict, he made himself available to coworkers who were losing their battle with drug addiction. He spoke frankly with others about their drug problems and let them know addictions can be overcome. Those persons who showed an interest he took to the treatment center where he had made a new start. In every way he could, he supported others in their battle for sobriety. The result was that coworkers often requested him as their working partner. One said, "Working alongside him for a day is like an eight-hour AA [Alcoholics Anonymous] meeting!"

6. A Person's Response to God's Call from History

There is a very basic conviction in an understanding of Christian vocation that God calls out of history. This history is twofold: one's personal history and the history of one's people.

God calls through personal history. This personal history includes many things: the family, nation, place, and culture in which I was born, all of which have a part in forming me. The gifts with which I was endowed, the opportunities I was given are part of my personal history from which God calls. The experiences of my life—joys, sorrows, tragedies, discoveries—have widened my awareness and contributed to who I am. God's call upon my life will be in the light of, and in harmony with, my personal history.

God calls out of the history of the times as well. Basically the message is: God is at work in the world; come and join God! This is the summons that Moses received from God. Deeply concerned about the oppression of people in Egypt, God called Moses to be the means of delivering them. For those with eyes to see and ears to hear, similar calls come out of the history of our times as well. William Overholt writes:

God is at work in our times and in our midst wherever the ministry of reconciliation takes place, wherever [people] strive for justice and freedom, whenever the ministries of medicine and education go forward, whenever gentleness, unselfishness and compassion replace lustful power, selfishness, and hardness of heart. This is what scripture and church have always said God was doing. This is what the Christian affirms that God *is* doing among us.

To make a vocational choice in our time is to say "yes" to what God is doing and to resolve to respond by enlisting in what [God] is doing to meet the needs of a desperate world.[9]

7. One's Response to God's Call from the World's Needs

Closely related is our seventh discovery—that God calls to us out of the needs of our world. John R. Mott, a missionary leader of another generation, was once asked what constituted a call to Christian service. Mott replied, "A need known and capacity to meet that need; that constitutes a call."[10] Those seeking to be more in touch with their total religious vocation may ask the same questions. What needs (personal, family, church, community, societal, national, or world) touch me? What personal gifts, large or small do I have to offer in the face of those needs?

8. A Response That Fits One's Gifts and Interests

A friend with whom I (Dick) discussed these matters offered me an important caution. I read the Overholt quote cited above, and she responded, "You just made me feel very guilty! I am hoping to be a performing artist. My fiancé plans a business career in sales management. In our work, neither of us will do much about 'the needs of a desperate world' as you put it. Do you think that our career plans are religious enough?"

I responded that their career plans seemed fitting from my perspective. I knew they would be caring, just people. I knew also that their choices fit them and they would do them well. In some way—whether in the workplace, in their citizenship or volunteerism roles, or in their financial gifts—they would make their contribution. Entertaining, creating beauty, and managing a business in a just, honest way are certainly Christian callings. Listening to the call from the world's needs does not mean that everyone will be a social crusader or a missionary. I hope my answer reassured her.

Actually, that was an incomplete answer. There are many ways of living out one's vocation. Years ago, Ernest Ligon, in his character research project, created a document titled "In Search of a Vision for Your Life." He suggested several broad areas of Christian calling:

1. To help the suffering. . . .
2. To create the beautiful. . . .
3. To discover new truths. . . .
4. To provide entertainment. . . .
5. To help young people become their best selves. . . .
6. To express my imagination. . . .
7. To make right prevail. . . .
8. To excel. . . .
9. To create a successful marriage. . . .
10. To give everyone . . . full opportunity to do [his or her] best. . . .
11. To make religion a power in [people's] lives.

William Overholt offers a similar list of possible callings:

1. To humanize urban life [as well as other conditions]. . . .
2. To seek world peace. . . .
3. To expand literacy and medical service, education and housing. . . .
4. To recover a standard of excellence, a style and purpose in art, music, literature, and drama. . . .
5. To expand the ecumenical and cosmopolitan spirit.[11]

There are many nuances of Christian vocation with places of connection and fit between each person's unique gifts.

9. Discernment of Unique Opportunities

A person's call comes through one's own uniqueness and the uniqueness of the times in which one lives. Viktor Frankl once said that to ask the question "What is the meaning of life?" is like asking a master chess player, "And now tell me, Maestro, what is the best move in chess?" Of course, one can give no general answer. Rather, the chess master's appropriate response would be, "A chess player must attempt, within the limits of the player's ability and within the limits imposed by his or her opponent, to make the best move at any given time."[12] Frankl is saying that the chess player must consider two factors: the strength of one's own position and the problem one faces. This provides one a clue in discerning one's vocation. One should consider the same two factors: first, one's unique capabilities, interests, ways of coping, values, and aspirations; second, the time in history in which one has been placed, its problems, its opportunities.

There was a time when the future looked very dark for the Jewish people. At that moment, Mordecai asked Esther, "Who knows? Perhaps you have come to royal dignity for just such a time as this?" (Esther 4:14b). Each person's vocation will occur within his or her own gifts and the uniqueness of the times.

10. Listening and Responding to the "Still, Small Voice"

Each of us needs to be aware that God has many ways of communicating with us if we are but aware, will listen and receive. God speaks in a number of "small voices." There are the small voices of symbols, dreams, persistent images in one's mind and heart, ideas, insights, and prayers. God speaks through inner reflections. The Bible describes many times when God has spoken to a person through such means. Such communication with God may continue today if we are open. Throughout one's life journey, it is important to pay attention to one's inner life, prayer life, and dreams.[13]

A part of our process of discerning Christian vocation is the cultivation of inner spiritual disciplines. It is to ask, Which of my inner thoughts and meditations are of God? What in my dreams (whether day or night dreams) may contain part of God's call for me? The Bible reminds us that God calls both from history and world needs and from within.

Roy Lewis also points out how vitally important it is to see this matter through. When our faith-value-meaning system is not congruent with our work, we may experience continuing stress, frustration, and dissatisfaction. This will be felt both in a person's work life and spiritual life. When vision is born within and one can see what one is to do in response to God's call, a wholesome congruence will come to one's life.[14]

BENEFITS FROM THIS FAITH PERSPECTIVE

We have been describing the Christian teaching of vocation as a way of understanding oneself and one's place in the world. This comprises a basic philosophy of life, one response to the search expressed in the opening paragraphs of this chapter.

When one understands life this way, there are some real advantages. James Fowler notes these consequences of such an understanding:

1. "In vocation we are called to an excellence that is not based upon competition with others."
2. We are thus freed to recognize and rejoice in the gifts and graces of others. We trust God for a certain "ecology of gift-edness."
3. We are freed from an anxiety that someone will "get there" before we do.
4. We are freed from the feeling of having to be all things to all people. We can experience our limits as gracious limits.
5. We are able to seek a responsible investment of our time and energy. We are released from workaholism. And then, we are able to enter more fully into work, family, education, culture, government, faith community, leisure, than we might otherwise have been.
6. We may be freed from the tyranny of time. We are called into life and called into death. We are accountable for the wise use of the time entrusted to us.
7. We become able to see vocation as "dynamic, as changing its focus and pattern over time, while continuing as a constant, intensifying calling." As we move through our life stages, some aspects of our vocation will change and emerge with time.[15]

Christian vocation is, therefore, a basic way of understanding life with all of its treasures and all of its opportunities.

MEANING FOR PARENTS

We have been exploring the basic Christian teaching about vocation and its implications for each person. This teaching can influence parents in many ways. To begin, we offer the following.

1. How Do I See/Interpret Myself?

Each parent will want to ask, "How do I orchestrate vocation in my own life? And how can I interpret this to my children?" Don't make those questions harder than they need to be! We are talking about basics here. Each parent has work, a family, a faith community and/or other communities, causes, interests, and concerns. Why are you doing what you are doing? Why are you doing these and not other things with your time? What do you hope for, dream for, in this round of activities? Your answers describe your vocation.

I (Dick) never spoke to my widowed mother in these terms. Still, I clearly knew her vocation. Her vocation was parenting—according to the beliefs, values, and dreams with which she and my father had founded their family. What is your vocation? Will your children recognize it as they look back upon their early years? In communicating this concept to our children, we start with ourselves.

2. Less than We Imagine

When we move from this self-examination and explore this with our children, we discover another insight: vocational guidance is less than we might have imagined. We do not have to help our children choose their precise occupations. No one is wise enough to do that. Even if we were that wise, no one can see all that the future holds for individuals and society. Our children's occupations will develop with their increasing competence and with the demands and opportunities of their times. What we need to help our children discover is more general than that— at least for the present.

3. More than We Imagine

However, the other side of that statement is that parental vocational assistance of children is thus also more than people might imagine. Children do not need to be led to a precise occupation. However, they do need to discover who they are in relation to the world and their Creator. In addition to fulfilling their children's needs for food, finances, clothing, and transportation, parents need to explore some basic questions with their children, including:

- What are the beliefs, convictions, passions, values, for which this family stands, which we invite you, our child, to consider?

- What unfinished tasks and unsolved problems do we as adults bequeath to our children?

- What are the present competencies and potential skills of this child? And what, in our family explorations, have we discovered to be his or her weaknesses? (These are opportunities for growth!)

- What (people and subjects) is this child concerned about, and how can she or he discover possible ways to act on these concerns?

In open continuing dialogue about such issues, the child may come to gain basic understandings of his or her present and future vocation. This will be a beginning of a topic that will continue to emerge throughout a lifetime.

4. Present and Future

Furthermore, a child's vocation embraces both the present and the future. For the present, a child's vocation is to be a child! The child must be allowed that. Adults can feel free to delight in the "childness" of their children. In far too many ways we busy ourselves and crowd out our children; then we hurry them along and miss them when they leave! Time to play, to dream, to imagine, to experiment, to question, to wonder, to laugh, to sing—these are the rights and needs of each child. This is the vocation of the child.

Parents may stand quietly by, pondering these things in their hearts. They may have some hunches about the meaning and direction of the child's experiences. However, they must learn an important truth. If parents push something on a child, the child will probably resist it. Children want the privilege of making their own discoveries. The call they hear themselves, on their own, is the one that feels authentic and real to them. Parents need the patience and the wisdom to allow children to listen for that call.

5. Joy and Hope in the Present and Future Child

To speak of vocation to our children is to express the joy and hope in what they can become. In this regard, we parents might learn something from John Erskine, who was once called "the greatest teacher Columbia University ever had." Erskine himself had many gifts and achievements—educator, concert pianist, author of sixty books. But, some said, his teaching was the best part of what he did. His wife, Helen, wrote that he was successful as a teacher because of two qualities. One was his "defiant optimism," and the other was "his own excitement for learning and his trust in the future." She recalled that he would often say to her, "Let's tell our young people that the best books are yet to be written; the best paintings have not yet been painted; the best governments are yet to be formed; the best is yet to be done by *them*."[16]

6. A Belief with Great Urgency

It is a matter of importance and urgency to invite our children into a discovery of their vocations. The world needs the creative imagination, the idealism, the strong commitments of children and youths. What a mistake it is to think that anyone's effort is not needed.

7. Trust in Childlike Faith and Discovery

We believe that children can hear God's call and can take steps to respond vocationally. A Bible story often told to children has to do with the child Samuel. This child heard repeatedly a quiet voice in the night. He finally recognized it (with the help of an adult) and responded, "Speak Lord, for your servant is listening" (1 Sam. 3). Children are so vulnerable that we adults must be careful not to manipulate them. Still, with honesty and integrity we can provide opportunities where they may come to hearing and discovery. We can provide these opportunities by:

- Helping children learn about models of the kind of living, caring, and competence that they would like to imitate.

- Exposing children to individual needs, community needs, together with some way to make an appropriate response.

- Introducing children to people who have achieved competence or artistry in activities or topics that interest them.

- Increasing children's awareness of their own growing abilities.

In these ways, children can begin to experience the gracious and gentle calling of God. They can begin their vocational journey of becoming.

In Conclusion

We have now shared Judeo-Christian teachings on vocation as a way of life. This view's implications for the spiritual guidance of children have been explored.

Your faith perspective may not be identical to ours—that is all right. Think through what you do believe about these matters, and then spell out their implications for life choice. Discover what this says to you about what you communicate to your children. Discern what is the heart of your faith that you want to communicate to your children. Think about how faith impacts your deciding, living, and working. Find ways to set an example and witness about this to your offspring as well.

By all means think, pray, and meditate through these issues. Find a way to share your convictions with your children. We all need some perspective on these matters to make our loving vocational support of our children complete.

A basic view of Christian vocation for ourselves and our children undergirds everything of which we speak in the following chapters. We now turn to specific ways to encourage that discovery.

P
A
R
T

2

VOCATIONAL DEVELOPMENT THROUGH THE YEARS

A vocation is not a once-and-for-all call. . . . It is a life-long conversation with God. Like any rich conversation, it is patterned by periods of spirited exchange, times of strain and argument, and intervals of silence. In such a developmental vision of a vocation, fidelity is more than memory. To be faithful entails more than re-calling an early invitation; it requires that we remain in the conversation. Our fidelity must be mobile because the conversation continues.

In this lifelong conversation with God we continue to hear hints and rumors of who we might become, of what we are to do. Only gradually over many decades do we come to glimpse what God imagines our life might become. Testing our insights and hopes against our abilities and environment, we very gradually come into our vocations. A vocation is thus not a mystical or abstract notion; it is the changing shape of our adult lives as Christians.[1]

In this section, we explore that conversation with God, a dialogue of self-discovery from infancy through young adulthood. Of course, vocational discovery is lifelong. To help our children, we need to be working on our discovery at the same time. The unique readiness and opportunities of each age are noted. The opportunities for families to contribute to a person's unfolding vocational discovery are offered and described.

Possible Road Map for Reading Part 2.   You may want to select the chapter (4–7) that describes your oldest child and read that first. Then you may want read about younger children or your child's earlier years. Chapter 8 enriches awareness by reporting experiences and suggestions of many vocational counselors who are also parents.

4

Early Childhood

A vivid two-scene memory sticks in my (Dick's) mind. The first scene was the day my wife and I brought our first baby home from the hospital. This was the first week-old infant I had ever held—our baby.

This excitement lasted for about a half-hour. Then, I had to leave to go to work. I did not want to let her go and leave, but others were waiting for their turn with her. My mother-in-law consoled me, "Don't worry, Dick. There will be plenty of time for that."

The second scene was nearly eighteen years later. Our family had taken our daughter to the university she had chosen to attend. Family members transferred her suitcases and boxes from the car to her dormitory room. As we drove reluctantly away, I remember wondering, "Where is that 'plenty of time' that my mother-in-law promised me?"

Out of that memory, vivid learning has come. One of the basic opportunities of parenthood is to claim the moment with each child. These moments are not just for providing food, clothing, shelter, and discipline. They are also for teaching, moral-spiritual guidance, and imparting vocational discovery. These moments are also for celebrating, enjoying, and affirming.

Furthermore, every parent needs to prepare one's child and oneself for an all-important day. That is the day when the parent will drive off (or the child will) as the young adult son or daughter begins independent living.

Let us then, examine the process of growth and development, beginning with early childhood. While there is tremendous variation from person to person, there are some common aspects in all persons' growth. These are stages of development. Erik Erikson has summarized these extremely well, and for the most part, we will follow his lead. We will note when females' life-stage issues are different from males'.

There are developmental tasks at each stage of life as well. These consist of the skills we need to acquire in order to master our environment and be ready for present and future tasks of living.[1]

There is also a central issue in each period of one's life, as well as a central process by which one deals with this central issue. All of this has significance for one's successful career choice and development. Barbara and Philip Newman have drawn together insights from many sources. For the most part, we will follow their lead on these topics.

We will summarize some of this information about life stages in each of the next four chapters. Remember, this is only a general summary. There may be any number of normal variations from it. With those cautions, let's reflect on early childhood and the important discoveries that occur there.

INFANCY—FROM BIRTH TO AGE TWO

The first two years of life is a time when learning and discovery take place at amazing speed. The infant has at least four developmental tasks in these two years. One is a development of social attachment—that is, an emotional tie with one's primary caregivers, parents and others. Another is to develop an understanding of means-ends relationship. That is, the child learns that some actions have certain effects on objects in one's environment. Still another is to develop a sense of "object permanence." The baby learns to comprehend that objects exist whether they or not they are in view. And another is the development of primary motor skills. At the beginning of this two-year period, the baby can hardly move. At the end, she or he can crawl, walk, run, eat, play, clap, and much more.

The central issue of this period of life is *trust versus mistrust.* An infant will show that this is being accomplished in the sense of comfort and trust with parents and other caregivers. Children know that they receive warmth, stimulation, consistency from their parents. At this stage in life, adults place few demands on children. So the issue is how effectively these adults meet the child's needs.

The process by which the child achieves this is the *mutuality* of child and caregiver. Every parent knows that this quality of care is not the parent's idea alone. Very early on, the child rewards fulfillment of this need with smiles, chuckles, and hugs. The child also makes it known when these needs are not being met! While children vary in their ability to call forth this caring behavior, all infants need this love and attention.

Stranger anxiety may occur at about seven months of age and separation anxiety at about nine months. The child shows great despair when the parents leave for a time. Repeated experiences often modify the intensity of the child's separation anxiety. The child discovers that parents exist even when they are not present.

The parent's task with the infant is to create as trustful an environment as possible. Trust in reliable human relationships will in turn lead to trust in one's environment—an important first step to appropriate vocational choice. It will also lead to trust in one's God. This trust plus an environment of love and prayer are the first contributions to the child's spiritual life.

In summary, the parent's role with their baby is to provide consistency and warmth so that the child's psychological, biological, and spiritual needs are met. This involves structuring the child's environment to be both stimulating and safe for the child in his or her rapid growth. And the parent needs to encourage exploration in the sensory, motor, and social areas of the child's environment.[2]

TODDLERHOOD—FROM AGE TWO TO FOUR

The most basic characteristic of this period of life is activity. Busyness, talking, moving, planning, and more occupy the child's time. At least four developmental tasks have been identified for children this age.

The first is the development of self-control. The child learns to control impulses. The child also needs to learn that she or he can influence other people and events. Toilet training begins in this period.

The second task is the development of language. By age four, a child typically has a vocabulary of one thousand words and can speak whole sentences. Language at this period is quite concrete though simple. It frees the child from depending on action alone to express feelings and influence others.

The third task involves fantasy and play. Both become much more elaborate for the toddler. In play and fantasy, the child may create characters and situations that have very private meanings for the child alone. Through imagination and play, small children can control situations beyond what they can in present reality. For example, they can punish and forgive, heal or inflict pain, conquer fear—all in their own interior world.[3] At this stage, some children develop an imaginary friend. This is probably the most elaborate form of fantasy for a child of this age and is a valuable experience for the child. This imaginary friend might be a companion when no one else is available, someone with whom to discuss impulses and right and wrong.

The fourth task is the further development of movement skills. During this time, children change from "toddlers" to skilled walkers and runners. The child may also love to swim, ski, skate, go sledding, and dance. She or he may begin to learn sports. A tricycle may come into a child's life. This leads to the fun of physical movement, the thrill of danger and independence, and the responsibilities that go with greater mobility.[4] These "wheels" also begin the child's increased independence from family and identification with peer group.

The central issue of this period of life is *autonomy versus shame and doubt.* Children become aware of their differences from their parents, and they want to test whether this is okay. At the beginning, the child uses rather primitive means to establish this autonomy or independence. These years are called the "terrible twos" with reason! A child may repeat the word "no," and the phrase "I do it," or be demanding and insist on having his or her own way. These are some of the early strategies in seeking personal autonomy. It may seem to parents that a lovable baby has become a monster! Parents need to realize that these are essential experiments for the child. One needs boundaries but also a sense of control and privacy. This contributes to a feeling of well-being. Such a child needs to know what one can control and what one cannot. The child also needs to know that it is all right to try to influence things and that, at least some of the time, he or she will succeed.

A child will endure long, slow struggles to put on pajamas or tie shoes. There will also be equally long rituals before going to bed and constant self-assertions of "I can do it myself." All of these are part of a child's struggle for autonomy. Parents naturally hope that the child will discover there are others' needs to consider as well. Parents need also to let the child to know that it is okay to be himself or herself. The goal is to allow the child adequate opportunity to experiment with autonomy. Hopefully, then, the child will have a foundation of self-confidence, paired with a delight in behaving independently.[5] While this may test parental patience when the child is three, there is a payoff. A son or daughter who is still a self-starter at twenty three has a much greater chance of success in education and in a career!

This search for autonomy will certainly result in periods of anger for both the child and those around the child. Parents will need to begin to communicate the sensitive message that it is okay to be angry. Children will need also to learn to express anger through channels that will not harm themselves, other persons, or valuable property.

The basic process by which children accomplish this is imitation. Once toddlers succeed in imitating a given skill, that skill belongs to them to use as they like. Many young children take to this quite naturally—they are incurable imitators. They will imitate others' behavior or walk. They repeat words they hear in conversations, on television, and in stories. If one child in a group makes a funny noise, all the others will want to try it. By mimicking and imitating, children vastly expand their range of possible behaviors.[6]

Such is the exciting growth in years two to four!

WHAT SIGNIFICANCE DOES ALL THIS HAVE FOR THEIR VOCATIONAL FUTURE?

These years are the very early part of what vocational psychologists call the "exploratory stage," and that it is. If our newborn infants who so

quickly become toddlers could express their questions to us, they might say this:

"It's going to be a long time before I can take care of myself. Who is going to care for me? Who will keep me warm and cuddle me? Who will feed me and give me something to drink? Will it feel loving and caring while you do that? Do you want to be there with me? Will you always be with me? If you must leave, will you see to it that a real caring person is there with me for as long as I need you?

"Who am I, and what is that world out there? Am I free to explore it—all of it? Is it okay to be curious? Can I discover parks and flowers and pets and stones? May I put them in my mouth? Is it okay to explore my own body? Is it all right to ask questions about God? Will you pray with me and tell me about loving people? Will you help me discover all sorts of things and get hurt as little as possible? When something frightens me, will you help me overcome my timidness or fear?

"I want to find out all the things I can do. May I climb and jump and talk lots without making you angry at me? May I keep trying to do something new even when you tire of waiting for me? When I get frustrated at trying to do something and throw it or hit it, will you help me?

"Do you know some parts of this world that I don't? If so, will you show them to me? Can I discover your music, your perfume, and the place where you work? I'll bet that's a fun place for girls and boys!

"When we have arguments, will you let me win some of the time? You see, I'm still young and I don't know what I can manage with other folks yet."

In a speech to early-childhood educators, Dr. Gary Landreth, a child therapist, offered "Rules of Thumb for Rearing Responsible Children." Some of his points underscore themes of this chapter. He observed that parents are either thermometers or thermostats. It is preferable to be a thermostat and *create* a climate rather than merely *record* the climate. He suggested that in creating a climate there are four growth-promoting messages to a child: (1) "I am fully here with you"; (2) "I hear you" (not listening to a child can make the child feel insignificant); (3) "I want to understand you"; and (4) "I care about you and your world."

He recommended further, "Don't try to straighten the bean sprout." In other words, let children grow at their own rate. He cautioned that words should not harm a child's self-concept and suggested instead,

"Focus on the doughnut, not on the hole. The doughnut is what is there. The hole is what is missing."

He followed that with a commonsense suggestion: "When a child is drowning is not the time to teach the child to swim." Parents need increasing wisdom to know when to intervene in a child's struggles and when to stay out. He concluded, "Listen to children with eyes, not only with ears."[7] We will add a few other specific suggestions to Dr. Landreth's wisdom on encouraging growth in children.

Returning to our earlier subject, it is impossible to overemphasize the importance of play for the child. There are schools of thought who say that play is the only basic need of a child beyond food, clothing, and shelter. Play is essential to becoming a whole person. Play and work are one in the child's mind—play is the child's work. And so it is important to allow and encourage play and enter into it with the child. The child will bring the willing adult into some aspects of play, perhaps awakening the parent's playfulness in ways that had been dormant for years. I (Dick) remember taking my daughter for a walk around the yard one spring. She wandered over to some tulips and started peeking inside the flowers. I got down on my knees and looked inside tulips with her. What a beautiful, fascinating world my child opened to me! Play may be the child's door to discovering Christian vocation in time. The things children delight in may have present and future connectedness to their call.

The adult may be able to suggest other play opportunities that will broaden the child's world. One such activity can be a type of imitation or identification in which the child joins the adult in "work" around the home. The child may enjoy dusting or making beds with a parent. One of my (Helen's) treasured snapshots is of my young son standing on a picnic bench, hanging clothes on the line to dry. That was play for him. My part was to encourage and accept his contribution.

At some time in these years, children may play their first games, perhaps board games. If parents are wise, they will postpone competition in these games for quite some time. They can enjoy the game for the shared activity it is.

Another topic of importance is that of television. Parents will want to decide if television is contributing to their child's growing world or preventing the child's discovery. They may want also to observe if watching television is becoming a substitute for other activities. How much and what programming is enriching for the child? Overdosing on television encourages passivity. This trend may start very early. Children need to be held and read to. Stories of faith heritage and stories of people to admire should be part of the reading diet.

In summary, the essential elements in a child's vocational development are increasing self-esteem and confidence, the child's growing world, and a sense of trust and joy.

Shortly, we will explore the issues of day care and preschool. Whether or not you elect those alternatives, the following little essay by Robert Fulghum highlights the significant discoveries of persons in this age group. Although he entitles his book *All I Ever Really Needed to Know I Learned in Kindergarten,* its subject is really preschool.

Most of what I really need to know about how to live, and what to do, and how to be, I learned in kindergarten. Wisdom was not at the top of the graduate school mountain but there in the sandbox at nursery school.

These are the things I learned: Share everything. Play fair. Don't hit people. Put things back where you found them. Clean up your own mess. Don't take things that aren't yours. Say you're sorry when you hurt somebody. Wash your hands before you eat. Flush. Warm cookies and cold milk are good for you. Live a balanced life. Learn some and think some and draw and paint and sing and dance and play and work every day some.

Take a nap every afternoon. When you go out into the world, watch for traffic, hold hands and stick together. Be aware of wonder. Remember the little seed in the plastic cup. The roots go down and the plant goes up and nobody really knows how or why, but we are all like that.

Goldfish and hamsters and white mice and even the little seed in the plastic cup—they all die. So do we.

And then remember the book about Dick and Jane and the first word you learned, the biggest word of all: LOOK. Everything you need to know is in there somewhere. The Golden Rule and love and basic sanitation. Ecology and politics and sane living.

Think of what a better world it would be if we all—the whole world—had cookies and milk about 3 o'clock every afternoon and then lay down with our blankets for a nap. Or if we had a basic policy in our nation and other nations to always put things back where we found them and cleaned up our own messes. And it is still true, no matter how old you are, when you go out into the world, it is best to hold hands and stick together.[8]

When families have adequately participated with the children in the processes we have described, there is reward. This reward is that the child is ready for the next adventure—the school years. Children will vary in the way they express this readiness, but they all will have discovered that it is okay to be who they are, to be different from their parents and from other children. They will be ready for a larger, more structured world.

QUESTIONS AND ANSWERS

Question: I am a mother with a career, and I have three months' maternity leave when my baby is born. Will I damage my child's sense of trust by having someone else care for the child during the daytime? Is child care that damaging? Would care by the child's father be better?

Answer: Responses to your question are widely discussed and debated. As regards care by fathers, there seems to be agreement that early literature about being deprived of the mother ignored the father. A constant, present parent can be either the mother or the father.

As regards child care, one woman investigated mothers who work outside the home and decided this was a good thing for both parents and children. She advised all such mothers to stop reading pediatric literature, which was apt to make them feel guilty for seeking child care for their children! She advises that if one is going to use child care, start it as early as possible, so that it becomes a part of the child's life.[9] Of course, others dissent and advise avoiding child care if possible.

Our feeling is that career parents can be responsive to their child's need even in the first year of life if they: find good child care with strong, caring persons; feel good about the choices they have made to combine career and parenting; and are willing to give parenting their top priority in the time not devoted to career.

This is a dilemma that many parents share. Well over 70 percent of parents of children between the ages of six and seventeen have mothers working outside the home. At least 60 percent of the mothers of children under six are working outside the home.

Question: Then, how do I select day care that will provide what my child needs?

Answer: The first step is to decide what you and your child need. A parent needs to be in touch with his or her own highest values in child rearing to recognize them in a potential caregiver.

There may be a central "clearinghouse" of information in your community. This might be the YWCA, the United Way, or an organization specifically designed to serve this function. Such agencies will be able to provide information about available resources and offer suggestions to parents beginning this search.

There are at least three categories of day care: private homes, non-profit centers (often in churches), and commercial (often franchised) operations. Of these three types, one early-childhood specialist told us:

> I encourage a day care situation in a home. I think a child should spend his/her time in an environment that has a real kitchen, bedroom, living room, etc., instead of being in an institutional setting. My second preference would be a church run day care center. A nonprofit group will be more apt to have the child's welfare as their prime focus. In my community, I have not had good experiences with the franchised day cares. I have had children from those settings transfer to my preschool, and they really have to be rehabilitated. It scares me that so many children are spending these precious, formative years in that environment. Choose a situation for your child that will provide the kind of discipline that is most like your own. The day care provider will more than likely spend more waking hours with your young child than you will.

A fourth type of day care is emerging—day care at one's workplace. When such day care is well done, it may well offer great advantages. Parents and children can commute together. Parents are available if an emergency arises and can possibly join their children for lunch and some moments of play. The amount of time absent from each other will be decreased to the actual work hours. Some parents who want to combine employment and parenting may want to advocate for day care services at their places of work.

In each of these settings, the primary concern is the caregiver(s). Will this person create an atmosphere that is warm and caring? Will there be opportunity for the child to experience a growing world in this discovery period of his or her life?

Since this decision is so important, a parent needs a clear-cut strategy to make the best possible choice. The following steps outline that kind of strategy.

Step 1

Visit the day care by yourself. Go prepared with a list of questions such as the following:

1. Is the home or center licensed?
2. What is the training or background of the staff? How great is the turnover of staff?
3. What is the ratio of staff to children?
4. What are the entrance requirements, such as age, toilet training, etc.?
5. What are the procedures for handling illness or accident?
6. What hours is care available?
7. What is the daily activity schedule?
8. Are there opportunities for the child to choose activities as well as times to follow directions?
9. Are there opportunities for the child to be alone as well as in small groups?
10. Are there adequate policies concerning health, nutrition, and safety?
11. Are there adequate play facilities, both indoors and outdoors?
12. Are there both male and female caregivers and role models?

Step 2

Visit the day care setting with your child. Observe the interaction between your child and the staff. Are they warm and affectionate? Is there evidence of mutual joy and enjoyment? Are there varieties of toys and play equipment? Are there objects or activities that particularly capture the child's interests?

Step 3

Visit the day care setting after your child begins to attend. The facility chosen should have an open-door policy. Once the parent has chosen a facility, it is important to develop and maintain a partnership with the caregivers. This enhances the possibility of continuity between home and day care.

Question: My daughter is three years old. Do I best contribute to her development by spending my time with her? Or should I place her in a preschool for some of her time?

Answer: There are two perspectives from which to consider this question. One perspective is the need of the particular child. If she is an extrovert with enough socialization skills, nursery school might be fun but not necessary. However, if the child is an introvert, nursery school may provide the opportunity to develop socialization skills. This child may need a nursery school where she is encouraged (in a noncriticizing manner) to participate. Possibly, parents alone cannot provide the social integration into a peer group. Of course, the introvert child might feel forced. It might be wise to start with a brief experience, say two or three half-days a week.

Another aspect of the child's need is the developing of independence, the "loosening of apron strings." Sometimes this is a need for the parent as well. Preschool that meets for a few hours a week might help both the child and the parent ease into school years.

The other perspective is the practice of the community where one is located. Will a child's school peers have had preschool experience that may leave them highly prepared for school activities? In some communities, more than 80 percent of all children have preschool experience. Some of these children will have had three years in these activities. In other communities, this percentage will be much lower.

Whether or not parents choose a preschool, we highly urge them to take their children to Christian education activities, Sunday school, vacation church school, choir, etc. These activities not only contribute to children's growing social world, but they also open up to them the larger worlds of belief and faith community. We urge this from the earliest-age class available in your faith community.

Question: How do you find a preschool that can provide what fits a child's needs at that time?

Answer: Most of what we said about choosing day care applies here as well. In addition, this is the advice of one preschool educator:

> I am biased toward church or synagogue operated preschools. They *care* about the child and the family. They can offer less costly tuition because the school does not have high operating expenses. The building is provided by the faith community, and any profit is used to upgrade the program and equipment. Visit several schools when selecting one for you and your child. Ask to bring your child along. Look at the faces of the children. Do they look happy and content? Perhaps the most important focus of preschool is to make your child's first impression of formal education a happy one. If s/he asks each morning "Is this the day I get to go to school" you have succeeded![10]

Question: All of this about childhood development and child care is interesting. But does it have any significance for my child's ultimate faith, vocation, and career choices?

Answer: Indeed it does! Your child's sense of trust, cooperation, inner reliability, curiosity, and initiative are all developing in these years. The issue in infancy is "trust." This has profound connection to one's ability to trust, believe, and have a deep faith throughout life. The issue in young childhood is "autonomy." This, too, connects to the ability to believe and decide for oneself, to delight in what God is doing in one's own life. Enjoyment and encouragement of the child's play, imagination, and fantasy may well blossom into means by which God communicates with this child. These are important factors in wise vocational choice.

Question: What, then, specifically should I do with my young children to encourage their development toward wise career decisions?

Answer: Enjoy your children and tell them so. Affirm your children. Laugh with them. Answer their questions and ask some questions of them. Encourage curiosity. Allow your children to join with you in any appropriate activity. Teach them the skills you use as they become able master these skills. Invite your children to go with you to places they might find interesting. Give your children as wide a range of experiences as possible. Do your best to provide an atmosphere of faith and love. Pray with and for your children. Tell them stories of your faith. But don't rush or push. This is a period of discovery.

5

Childhood in the School Years

As children enter into the school world, new tasks and issues await them. As we begin, let's pause for two relevant parables. Here's the first.

Once a little boy went to school. It was quite a big school, but when the boy found he could go right to his room from the playground outside he was happy, and the school didn't seem quite so big anymore. One morning when the little boy had been in school for a while, the teacher said, "Today we are going to make a picture."

"Good," thought the little boy. He liked to make pictures. He could make lions and tigers and trains and boats. He took out his crayons and began to draw. But the teacher said, "Wait. It's not time to begin." And she waited until everyone looked ready. "Now," said the teacher, "we are going to make flowers."

"Good," thought the little boy, and he began to make beautiful flowers with his orange and pink and blue crayons. But the teacher said, "Wait." She drew a picture on the blackboard. It was red with a green stem. "There, now you may begin."

The little boy looked at the teacher's flower. He liked his better, but he did not say this. He turned his paper over and made a flower like the teacher's. It was red with a green stem.

On another day the teacher said, "Today we are going to make something with clay." "Good," thought the little boy. He could make all kinds of things with clay—snakes and snowmen and elephants and mice—and he began to pinch and pull his ball of clay. But again the teacher said, "Wait. I will show you how." And she showed everyone how to make one deep dish. The little boy just rolled his clay in a round ball and made a dish like the teacher's. And pretty soon he didn't make things of his own anymore.

And then it happened that the little boy and his family moved to another city and the boy had to go to another school. On the very first day he went to school the teacher said, "Today we are going to make a picture." "Good," thought the boy and he waited for the teacher to tell him what to do. But the teacher didn't say anything. She just walked around the room. When she came to the boy she said, "Don't you want to make a picture?"

"Yes," said the boy. "What are we going to make?"

"Well, I don't know until you make it," said the teacher.

"How should I make it?" said the boy.

"Why, any way you like!"

"And any color?"

"Any color," said the teacher. "If everyone made the same thing in the same color, how would I know who made what and which was which?"

"I don't know," said the boy, and he began to draw a flower. It was red with a green stem.[1]

Here's the second parable:

The animals came together and decided to form a school. There was a bird, a squirrel, a rabbit, a gopher, and a fish on the board of education. The gopher insisted that burrowing be in the curriculum for everyone. Likewise the bird wanted flying, the rabbit wanted running, and the squirrel wanted to include perpendicular climbing. And the fish insisted that all should be taught to swim. In the curriculum guide, they insisted that all of the animals take all of the subjects. Rabbits were achieving A's in running, but when attempting climbing, they became injured. Soon, they were not running well either. Birds flew beautifully but couldn't burrow very well. They broke their beaks and injured their wings until they were making C's in flying and F's in burrowing. Eventually, the valedictorian of the class was an unenthusiastic eel who did everything in a halfway fashion! However, the animal board of education was happy. Everyone was taking all the subjects in what they termed a broad-based education.[2]

Educators tell such stories among themselves as they critique and improve their institutions. Such stories may also be helpful to parents as their children enter those institutions.

Schools will be the most prominent influence for at least the next twelve to thirteen years of the youngster's life. These schools will make enormous contributions to the person's vocational-occupational development. Yet they are not perfect. And so the parent may need to help the child adjust to the school and the school be responsive to the child. Let's explore this in more detail. We first look at the early school years.

EARLY SCHOOL AGE—AGES FIVE TO SEVEN

By age five, school is no longer a family option—it is a requirement. Both parents and children may admit to butterflies in their stomachs on the first days of school. The child is leaving the safety and comfort of home for a long period each day. To a small child, the school building may appear to be huge, strange, and scary. Although a child may have some idea of what school will be like, there is much that is unknown that the child will need to face without mother or father. Even if the child attended preschool or day care, the new school may be a large, strange new experience. There may be more and older children to whom to adjust.

For the parent, there is a parallel adjustment. School is that time when others begin to "take over" the raising, teaching, discipline, and evaluation of one's child. (Again, for many, this will be a continuation of influences from day care or preschool.) There will be even more sources of influence. Family beliefs and practices may well be scrutinized and challenged. More-objective adults will evaluate and reality test the abilities and performance of the child.

The family is now joined by school, the child's peer group, and the neighborhood as sources of influence on the child. Television and other media will also continue to be influences. The child may respond with a wide-ranging curiosity covering all facets of life and existence. The independence of action that we noted in the toddler is supplemented by independence of thought in these early school years.[3]

There are at least four developmental tasks for the five- to seven-year-old child. The first is developing an adequate sex-role identification. This involves: learning of the gender label (I am a boy, I am a girl); establishment of the sex-role preference (I like being a boy, I like being a girl); and identification with the same-sex parent (I want to be like Daddy, I want to be like Mommy, or other important adults). Probably most of us agree with this description of sex-role identification to this point.

However, students of human development suggest there is yet another component—the "acquisition of the sex-role standards." The Newmans offer such examples as "Males are 'independent,' 'achievement oriented,' 'assertive.' . . . Females are 'interpersonal,' 'care givers,' 'docile.'"[4] Parents may well ask, "Do we want our children to accept what culture often says about male and female behavior roles? What do we want to teach and model for our children? What other adults, literature, and media would we like to bring into our child's experience to help him or her feel freedom as regards sex roles? Do we want our child to feel locked into occupational choices that are perceived as traditionally male or female? If not, we will make sure they meet persons in occupations not usually associated with their gender." In the next chapter, we will consider possible bias against girls in school.

In order to help our child, we parents may need to ask more sensitively, "What does it mean to be male? to be female?" We have some different body parts, and we have different roles in child conceiving and bearing. Are there other differences that appear real to us and that we want to pass to our children? As adults, we want to claim, enjoy, and be comfortable with our gender. Furthermore, we should be clear about the freedoms we claim for ourselves in regard to our gender. In this way, we can help our children begin to claim similar gender clarity.

A second developmental task is "early moral development." From infancy, the child has heard some behaviors encouraged and some discouraged or forbidden. Until this time in a child's life, those influences felt external. Now the child begins to develop beginning concepts of moral behavior. Parents have consciously and unconsciously communicated what they believe to be right and wrong. They have rewarded some behaviors and punished others. Children have heard some other statements of right and wrong at church, in school, on television, and from friends. Perhaps the child has also learned empathy for others.

In all of this, the child's conscience begins to develop. An active part of any conscience is the feeling of guilt. The sensitive parent may well ask, "What seems to produce guilt in my child? Is that fitting, appropriate guilt? Is the child overburdened with guilt? Is it stifling the child's curiosity and initiative?" This is an opportunity for the parent with faith and vocational sensitivity. It may be time to share beliefs about forgiveness. It may also be a time to begin teaching about opportunities to address wrongs in our society and world. To help the child move from a too-heavy guilty conscience to an active social conscience is an important contribution.

The child may be actively curious about sensitive areas, such as another person's body, sexual information, sexual orientation, reproduction, or previously unchallenged family beliefs. Parents may need to discover how to respond to such curiosity without making the child feel, "I am bad for wanting to know about that."

A third developmental task involves "concrete operations"—the ability to understand some basic principles as to how one's world works. The components include the following:

Conservation (understanding the constancy of physical matter in mass, weight, and volume).
Classification (ability to group objects according to common characteristics).
Combinatorial skills (ability to manipulate numbers, that is, to begin to do addition and subtraction, in anticipation of multiplication and division).[5]

These tasks represent an amazing rate of growth. The child is making a major shift toward adult thinking, using logic, classifications, and observational-organizational skills.

A fourth developmental task is group play. While continuing to use fantasy, children begin to have interest in group games that are more structured and oriented to reality. They learn to play games that are more complex and use increased physical skills.[6] Their play is moving in the direction of the structured team sports.

Such are the developmental tasks of early school age. The central issue for this stage of life is *initiative versus guilt.* Initiative is active inquiry and investigation of one's world.[7] This is similar to but different from toddlers' issue of *autonomy versus shame.* Toddlers seek their own inner right to autonomy while early school children address their outer world. They want to see if there is the same kind of reliability in this outside world as they have discovered inside themselves.

The child's central process is identification with parents. This includes taking desired characteristics of one's parents into oneself.

A child may experience some "bumps" in this exploration. Every culture has some taboos as to what is acceptable for a child to investigate and what is not. Incest is one of the taboos of our society. Some of us have more taboos than others. When a child senses that she or he has violated cultural or family taboos, the internal feeling is guilt, leading the child to question: "Am I good because I have such a driven curiosity about everything or am I bad? Should I go on investigating or should I stop?" Such is a central issue for this age. We encourage setting children free to utilize all the initiative and curiosity they want. It is healthy for them and has rich rewards in career discovery.

Having successfully resolved these all important tasks and life issues, the child is ready to begin the next stage of development.

SCHOOL AGE, YEARS EIGHT THROUGH TWELVE

These are years of great intellectual growth, competence, and development. There is growing investment in work. Children are learning the fundamental skills their culture expects of them to survive and to contribute. They also develop some realism as to their greater and lesser skills. At this time, children make their first commitments to a social unit that is larger than the family. This is a time of growth in task skills, in social skills, and in emotional development.

Eight- to twelve-year-old children need to master at least four developmental tasks. The first is learning even more social cooperation. This is likely to occur in the same-sex friendship group, in which a child gains an appreciation of the many points of view that may be present in that group. There may be several different versions of the same song, different ways to play the same game, different ways to celebrate the same holiday. The child will also become more sensitive to what it takes to belong to the group. Further, the child may discover the experience of intimacy with a non-family member, a person of his or her own age.

Second, there is the task of learning self-evaluation. With all the skills children hope to achieve, they will have a lively interest in knowing how they are doing. During this period, children will depend a good bit on their evaluation by others—both peers and adults. Children will rely on such evaluation experiences as report cards, teachers' comments, parental commendation, and friends' approval. If children are informed that important adults consider them cooperative, intelligent,

or creative, they will likely incorporate this into their own self concept.[8]

Third, there is skill learning. A most impressive aspect of these years is the acquisition of many skills—intellectual, artistic, and athletic.

Children grow in thinking skills during this time of their lives. The areas of science, history, and mathematics are now available to them. They can use the principles of classification, causality, measurement, hypothesis forming, and hypothesis testing. They become able to move beyond the limits of their own experience and to consider events that happened long ago as well as those that could happen in the future or in the present.

Probably the single most significant skill that the child masters in this period is reading. Having mastered reading, the child becomes capable of independent inquiry and of using a vast reservoir of resources. A skilled reader is able to expand his or her information, imagination, and skills. The importance of reading is impossible to exaggerate. If the child is having difficulty with reading, the best possible diagnosis, tutoring, and loving parental attention will be important investments in the child's future.

When a child has developed the ability to read, the parent has a rich faith opportunity—to provide exciting reading materials about faith and people of faith. When my (Dick's) grandson was excited about his new skill of reading, I gave him a simple first reader's Bible. How eagerly he consumed it, reading it through several times. In time, his reading skills matured and he was ready for yet other materials.

School children of this age can also gain complex art skills. They can also make and appreciate music at a more complex level.

Children make tremendous strides in their athletic abilities as well. They can master the coordination, timing, and concentration required for athletics, at least in elementary ways. The ability to begin to play almost every adult sport becomes possible in these years.

Still another developmental task is team play. Children begin to evolve a sense of team, club, membership. They are able to devote energy to team successes as well as personal success and to subordinate personal goals to group goals. They learn about cooperation and competition. They learn how to participate in group goals and to divide the labor with others. Parents cannot control all the choices a child makes concerning groups and teams. They can, however, be "quietly influential" in exposing their child to wholesome opportunities.

The central issue for children of this age is *industry versus inferiority.* Children gain a sense of industry by having an eagerness to master new skills and perform meaningful work. They discover aspects of work that are motivating and become fascinated with new skills, sensing that they are coming closer to the skills of adults. An increased sense of independence and self-worth may accompany this skill building.

How might a child develop a sense of inferiority? It might come from two sources: from the self (expecting too much from himself or herself and failing to meet those expectations); or from others. Failure or poor performance (or a lower level of performance than the parents expect) in school can contribute to a negative self-concept—inferiority.

Children may also have a sense of inferiority when they discover that they may be different from other children. Such children may also feel uncomfortable with what teachers and other adults expect. For example, an introverted child may have a slowness to develop social skills, a need for privacy, a slowness to share thoughts and responses, a tendency to drop the head and avoid eye contact. (On the other hand, the child may be totally energized by private reading projects and thinking). Unaware adults may see something wrong or inferior in such behavior and attempt to change the child. Caring parents may need to help the child and school officials to deal with each other in a sensitive way, accepting the child as is.[9]

Children need to learn that each person has some skills in which he or she is better than others. Each person will experience some success and some failure. Children also need to learn to accept themselves and others as they are.

The central process for dealing with this life issue is education. It is there, most of all, that one's industry will be recognized, affirmed, encouraged, and rewarded. It is in education that failures will feel most severe and contribute to negative self-image.

This is a period filled with important issues. One's self-concepts of industry, mastery, and achievement are all explored here. A child needs to develop an understanding of what success is and how one is successful. Social skills, cooperation, and interpersonal sensitivity are developed at this stage. A child may be discovering some potentially high and low skill areas. This will be important for eventual career decisions. All of these matters are of crucial importance to being an effective adolescent and adult.[10]

WHAT SIGNIFICANCE DOES ALL THIS HAVE FOR ONE'S VOCATIONAL FUTURE?

In these momentous years, a parent has opportunities to contribute to a child's future. The parent may be tempted to let go. Other authorities and experts have entered into the child's life: it is easy to feel threatened when the child's statements change from "mother says, father says" to "my teacher says. . . . " However, a parent is wise to overcome this temptation and recognize this as a necessary step in the child's growth. Parents can accept school and emphasize its importance. They can look forward with their child to this new adventure in life.

Children may have mixed feelings about surrendering their own freedom to school. It will be easiest for them if they do not also have to worry about their lonely parents at home.

The parents can take interest in, encourage, applaud each new gain in "initiative" and "industry." If parents love to read, they can make that clear to children. They can share some of their favorite readings. They can listen to the child read and read to the child. As a matter of fact, Gordon Lawrence suggests that reading aloud to someone is almost necessary for the vast majority of children in learning to read. He notes that 70 percent of all persons are extroverts, who "really do their best thinking with their mouths open."[11] Reading as a social activity will be most important for such a child. Reading together can be fun! Parents can give gifts of books that open up the realm of reading for pleasure and new experiences.

Furthermore, parents can be aware that their children are exploring many interests and possible skills. They can encourage each interest as it comes up. They can also let that interest go without regret, knowing that it may return at another time. Parents can be quite clear in their minds that the future belongs to the prepared. Therefore, without undue tension or pressure, they can encourage the joy that comes with mastering new skills and discovering new knowledge.

Parents can help their children come to grips with "reality testing" as teachers, peers, competition, winning, and losing expose the child to new information. Some of this information may be hard to accept. Others may not see the child as gifted as the family has. With home as a haven, children can learn to accept such evaluations. It may lead them to discover that some activities are not for them. They may need also to learn to try harder at some where they would like to excel.

Occasionally, children come to think of themselves as "dumb" in a topic or "not good" at a skill. This may not be true at all. Sadly, this can cut the child off from continuing to explore something that could be very interesting or rewarding. Since children vary so much in the rate of their maturation, a child may have encountered something before being personally ready for it. And since all of us vary at the speed with which we absorb knowledge or gain skills, one person may just take longer than another to get some things down. However, that person may be very good at that subject from then on. Therefore, it is a good idea for parents to conduct supportive investigation of any trouble spots a child might be experiencing.

These years are called the "growth stage" or the "fantasy phase." Remember, dreams, "fantasies,"—whether worthy or unworthy, day or night—may well be a vehicle of revelation, discovery, and guidance. It was true of Joseph in the Bible (Gen. 35–50). It may be true for your child as well. The child has ever-increasing skills to observe and absorb. There is an opportunity for parents to see how much of the world they can open up to their children. A child who plays a musical instrument would perhaps be stimulated by a concert by a gifted artist. A child who enjoys athletics would find good high school, college, or professional games rewarding. Attending a play—whether a high school, college, or professional production—might fascinate the child who likes drama. If the child has a feeling for others, a visit to care providers in nursing homes, hospitals, or homeless shelters might suggest future opportunities. The child who has an interest in growing things might be interested in a visit to a greenhouse or plant nursery. If the child has a curiosity about scientific matters, perhaps a visit to some lab or research facility might stimulate even more curiosity. The possibilities are endless. Don't miss the opportunity to let your child experience what you do and what it means to you. They could also visit other adults whom they like and admire in their workplaces.

Perhaps a personal recollection by famed author Budd Schulberg will help bring to life the excitement of these school-age years. He calls this story "My Wonderful Lousy Poem." He recalls, "When I was eight or nine years old, I wrote my first poem." At that time, his father was head of Paramount Studios in Hollywood, his mother a prime mover in bringing "culture" to their community.

He brought his poem to his mother, who cried over it and felt it beautiful beyond words. Buddy glowed with pride and eagerly awaited his father's arrival so he could show him the poem as well.

As he waited for his father, he wrote the poem out in his finest hand. Then he colored an elaborate border—to do justice to the brilliant content.

His father did not arrive on time. This was not unusual. His father was a hard-driven person whose job included many frustrations with the "temperamental artists" he worked with.

When his father finally arrived, he was shouting, "Imagine, we would have finished the picture tonight. Instead that moron suddenly gets it into her beautiful head that she can't play the last scene. So the whole company has to stand there at a thousand dollars a minute while this silly little [blank], who's lucky she isn't behind the counter of a five-and-ten, walks off the set! And now I have to beg her to come back on Monday!"

In the midst of this tirade, he saw the poem and picked it up. Buddy's mother told his father how wonderful this poem is. His father said he would decide for himself. After an agonizing silence, his father spoke, "I think it's lousy."

As Buddy's eyes were getting wet, his mother and father quarreled over the poem. He still remembers his father's self-defense, "Look, I pay my best writers two thousand dollars a week. All afternoon I've been tearing apart their stuff. I only pay Buddy fifty cents a week. And you're trying to tell me I don't have a right to tear apart his stuff if I think it's lousy!"

Buddy couldn't stand any more. He ran from the dining room. Up in his room, he threw himself on the bed and sobbed.

Eventually, family wounds healed. His father and mother began talking again. His father took him to a prize fight—his favorite form of entertainment. Buddy began "committing poetry" again, though not showing it to his father.

He recalls that a few years later he took a second look at that first poem and decided for himself that it was a pretty lousy poem. After a while, he worked up the courage to show his father something new. His father thought it was overwritten but not hopeless. Buddy was learning to rewrite. His mother was discovering that she could criticize him without crushing him. They were all learning. By now he was twelve.

As he looks back, he recalls:

> But it wasn't until years later than the true meaning of that painful "first poem" experience dawned on me. As I became a professional writer, doing books and plays and films, it became clearer and clearer to me how fortunate I had been to have a mother who said, "Buddy, did you really write this? I think it's wonderful!" and a father who shook his head no and drove me to tears with, "I think it's lousy." A writer—in fact every one of us in life—needs that loving-mother force from which all creation flows; and yet alone it is incomplete, even misleading, finally destructive, without the father force to caution, "Watch. Listen. Review. Improve."
>
> Sometimes you find these opposing forces personified in associates, friends, loved ones. But finally you must counterpoise these opposites within yourself: first, the confidence to go forward, to do, to become; second, the tempering of rampant self-approval with hardheaded, realistic self-appraisal, the father discipline.
>
> Those conflicting but complementary voices of my childhood echo down through the year—*wonderful . . . lousy . . . wonderful . . . lousy*—like two powerful, opposing winds buffeting me. I try to navigate my little craft so as not to capsize before either. Between the two poles of affirmation and doubt, both in the name of love, I try to follow my true course.[12]

As children progress through the grade-school years, taking lumps and developing initiative and industry, they will eagerly leap into the next life stage—adolescence. They seem to be doing that earlier all the time. They will probably be much more ready for that than their parents are!

QUESTIONS AND ANSWERS

Question: I don't know what to do about my son. He liked learning to read, all right. And now that's all he does! Any free time, he's in his room alone, reading. Should I be concerned?

Answer: That depends. If he loves reading and chooses to do that with his spare time, you have little reason for concern. You may be dealing with an "introverted intuitive" (see chapter 10) who prefers the world of concepts and ideals. Such a person needs time for contemplation before sharing thoughts or activities. If you encourage other types of activity, do so gently in a manner that is noncritical. However, if your son is hurt or afraid of other people or activities and so retreats into reading, perhaps he needs help to choose some additional activities. It's probably good to give this some time and see if his interests broaden out on their own.

Question: My son eats, drinks, and breathes competitive sports. I'm afraid attention to schoolwork suffers. He isn't interested in music or other activities to which I'd like to introduce him. Just sports, morning, noon and night. Playing them or watching them. Is there anything I can do but wait and hope?

Answer: It appears that your child operates primarily through extroversion and sensing. (Again, see chapter 10.) This combination of orientation to the outer world is seen in a desire for fun, action, and competition. Individuals with this combination also like organizing and responsibility. Sports provide these opportunities. Role models are important to them. You might be able to find some good athletes to give you a hand! Perhaps you could arrange to visit with a respected coach or athlete or a person who makes a living in a recreation occupation. These persons might help your son know what's involved in preparing to get to the level they have attained. And they might tell your son about their range of interests, giving him "permission" to be an athlete with wider interests.

Question: I agree with what you say about the importance of school.

Unfortunately, my daughter doesn't. We opened a savings account for her college education the week she was born. And we have always assumed that she would want a good education. However, from the first day of school, she has not wanted to go, held back, not enjoyed it, and not achieved. We are all so frustrated. Is there anything that we can we do?

Answer: We urge you to seek excellent educational-vocational testing and counseling for her and for you, her family. Perhaps this evaluation will reveal that your hopes for her are beyond her abilities. If so, love and accept her as she is. Help her find a place within her range of abilities where she can be happy. Perhaps you will discover that she has gifts but that present schooling somehow does not fit her. Either it does not provide a learning style that engages her or offers no opportunities in her fields of interest. If so, then you might be wise to spend some of that educational money on tutoring, private lessons, or a school that will provide what she needs.

Question: What does all this have to do with my child's eventual discovery of Christian vocation?

Answer: Much indeed. Here is a summary of at least some of the parental opportunities during these years:

- As the child develops a beginning moral sense and conscience, there is opportunity to communicate the values of one's faith. Care should be taken not to make this so heavy that the child is overwhelmed with guilt. At the same time, moral outrage at wrongs at home, in school, or in society should be encouraged. This has always been one of God's means of calling persons.

- With children's developing ability to read, parents are empowered to provide their children the opportunity to discover about faith and possible vocational expression for themselves.

- The child's initiative and curiosity can be welcomed and encouraged, including curiosity about belief and faith.

- A child's discovery that using one's developing skills to make others happy, such as by making a gift for someone, is a vocational contribution.

- Contributing to a child's sense of "industry" and doing all one can to avoid/overcome a child's sense of "inferiority" relates directly to the belief that all are created in God's image. It also relates to the strength with which one searches for vocation.

Certainly there is more. At least these opportunities exist for the child's developing experience of faith and vocation.

6

Youth in the Middle-High and Senior-High Years

Recently I (Dick) had opportunity to visit friends who teach, counsel, or administer in middle and senior high schools in my community. After spending several hours on these visits at their schools, my mind was filled with the images of those experiences:

- Physically mature young women, elegantly dressed, and equally mature young men, along with folk who haven't even started developing physically. . . .

- Disciplined musicians promptly arriving before seven for an hour's drill before school, and groups having one last smoke on the corner before deciding whether or not to ditch school for the day. . . .

- Beautiful art work and displays in halls that had trash everywhere. . . .

- Delicate classical music played skillfully in rehearsal rooms and cafeterias with rock music so loud that my ears hurt. . . .

- Faces filled with joy and hope and faces reflecting loneliness, struggle, or anger.

All of these widely varying images had one thing in common. They were all related to that five- or six-year period called early adolescence. This period of time is the bridge between childhood and adulthood.

66

It is no wonder that parents and youths find themselves confused about themselves and career decisions. We will provide some perspectives by exploring five questions:

1. What are the developmental tasks and the central issue for persons in this era of their lives?
2. What are the career tasks that young people need to face?
3. What are their post-high school options?
4. What are some basic issues that youths and their families face?
5. What can parents do to work with their adolescent children on these issues?

DEVELOPMENTAL TASKS AND CENTRAL ISSUE

Teenagers face at least four developmental tasks. Each of these is important to their spiritual and vocational development. The first task is to come to terms with physical maturing. The beginning of this stage of life is often marked by a rapid growth spurt. On the average, this generally peaks for females at age eleven and for males at age thirteen. However, there is amazing variety. Early maturing girls and boys may have to deal with persons who assume that they are older. Adults may expect them to take more responsibility and be ready for more-mature social experiences than they truly are. Slow-maturing girls and boys may have to live with just the opposite. In addition to an increase in height, early adolescents' reproductive systems mature, secondary sex characteristics develop, and body weight is redistributed.

This rapid physical growth and change has many effects. The changes bring adolescent persons closer to an image of themselves as adults. These changes strengthen their sexual identity. Such changes are apt to make them more self-involved, self-conscious, self-absorbed—at least for a time. And these changes are apt to evoke some mixed feelings in the young persons themselves.

In order for these young people to accept what is happening so quickly to them, they need adequate information about the meaning of these changes. They also need acceptance and a supportive atmosphere, in both family and peers.[1]

At this stage, a young person needs to realize, "This is a time to claim the Christian teachings about the goodness of all creation, including myself, my gender, my body, my sexuality." It is also a time to claim the biblical teaching about each person being in the image of God and therefore of infinite worth.

A second developmental task is the maturing of thought and reasoning. This is called "formal operations." It describes the growing ability to develop logical principles and apply them to thought processes and decisions.

New skills begin to emerge. The young person learns to juggle more than two groups of variables in one's head at the same time, to imagine changes in the future, to think and suggest ideas about a logical sequence of events that could possibly occur. At this stage, one develops the ability to anticipate the consequences of one's actions (at least some of the time). One also may be able to discover whether there is logical consistency or inconsistency in a series of statements. The teenage person may abandon some of the absolutes of childhood and see both sides of a wide variety of topics. These increasing capabilities need to be matched by opportunity and a challenge to think in a more complex way about faith, theology, social, and moral issues. Otherwise, the young person may receive a message that the Christian faith is only for children.

The third and fourth developmental tasks are closely related. They involve achieving membership in a group of friends and forming satisfying relationships with persons of both sexes. Adolescents will spend more time away from their homes. They will likely enjoy talking with their peers, in person or on the phone. They look to their group for companionship and fun as well as intimacy, support, and understanding.[2]

Popularity and acceptance into peer groups become an absorbing concern. This acceptance seems to be based on one or more of the following characteristics: looks, athletic ability, social class, academic performance, future goals, religious affiliation, ethnic group membership, or special talents.

Two things are going on at the same time in all this: finding those groups where one belongs and learning the necessary social skills. Teenagers want confidence that they can locate groups and individuals with whom they want to associate and that they can build relational bridges with those folks.

The central issue for persons of this age is *group identity versus group alienation*. The question is, "Who am I, and with whom do I belong?"

A young woman of middle high school age came to her father and tearfully exclaimed, "Dad, I think I'm smart in everything except what matters!" She was experiencing the central struggle of this era. Where is my relational savvy? How can I pick friends and establish closeness with them so I feel supported but still be myself? And if the "I as an individual" conflicts with the "I as a group member," which "I" do I surrender?

The parent can help a young person discover rich group experiences. A significant youth conference, mission service trip, or shared adventure (church or scout camp, etc.) may have a lasting impact.

This life issue is solved when the young person has found a group that meets his or her needs and provides a sense of belonging. (The solution may be temporary. It will come up again.) A negative resolution of this issue leaves the person with a sense of being alienated from the peer group. This may express itself in preferring older or younger people and in being uneasy around one's own age group.[3] If this sense of not belonging is strong enough, the young person may express it in drastic ways—for example by dropping out of school, living in isolation, engaging in antisocial behavior, or even despairing of life itself.

The issues of successful friendships, relationships, and group membership are always relative. Very few people feel completely successful in that regard. That knowledge in itself may be comforting. Still, it is extremely important to know how central and basic this issue is for middle-high and senior-high students. Someone once wrote, "Friendship doubles life's joys and halves life's sorrows." While that is always true as a life issue, for adolescents, it is *the* life issue.

The adolescents' central process for dealing with this issue is to open themselves up to the pressures and social influence of the group. "In most cases, adolescents' personal values are altered and shaped by peer group pressure in order to increase the similarity between themselves and the other group members."[4]

CAREER DECISIONS

In these years, young people continue to explore both themselves and possible work worlds. They are also beginning to narrow down those choices to the more appropriate and possible ones.

Vocational psychologist Donald Super notes how crucial these years are. He points out that in adolescence one begins a career "exploration stage" that will continue until about age twenty-five. Super notes that self-examination, role tryouts, and occupational exploration take place in school, leisure activities, volunteer activities, home, and part-time work. There are three substages:

1. *Tentative (ages fifteen to seventeen):* Needs, interests, capacities, values, and opportunities are all considered. Tentative choices are made and tried out in fantasy, discussion, courses, work.
2. *Transition (ages eighteen to twenty-one):* Reality considerations are given more weight as the young adult enters the labor market, military service, or higher education and attempts to implement a self-concept.
3. *Trial (ages twenty-two to twenty-four):* The person finds a beginning job or locates a seemingly appropriate field, and tries it out as a career decision.

Super notes there are also vocational developmental tasks in this life stage and the one following. (Actually, they cover a ten- to fifteen-year time period, beginning with early adolescence.) These must be accomplished in order to be ready for the next stage in one's career.

There are a series of five of these vocational developmental tasks. The first is crystallization of a vocational preference. This is a tentative, somewhat vague, choice of a general field of work. Crystallization is simply formulating some ideas as to possible fields and work levels and discovering what preparation is needed.

The second is specification of a vocational preference. One chooses a specific career from the general area one has chosen in the previous task.

Third is implementation of a vocational preference. One completes the training and begins to work at the task.

Fourth, there is stabilization in a vocation. One attempts to further one's self-realization by finding the right place within a chosen occupation. One may experience a period of trial and error, of moving from one job to another and employer to another. All too often, first jobs in a field are not all that satisfying! (Even when one feels "stable" in a career, there may well be subsequent changes throughout one's lifetime.)

Fifth, there is consolidation of status and advancement—growing and developing in ways that contribute to further progress and personal growth.[5]

Super observes further that persons choose their occupations through one or more of the following three processes:

1. *Identification:* That is, a person observes another person (consciously or unconsciously) and says, "I am like that person" or "I want to be like that person."
2. *Experience:* A person chooses some experiences and is cast into others by circumstances. Each activity reveals some strengths and some weaknesses also some attractions and some "turnoffs." These all aid in the decisions that gradually one will have to make.
3. *Observation:* Observing, reading, and hearing things that cause a person to think a given field inappropriate.[6]

(See Chapter 9 for a supplementary perspective by Hummel and McDaniel.)

OPTIONS AFTER GRADUATION

At the end of this time period, the young person will graduate from high school. Up to that point, his or her life script has been pretty well planned—school and more school. But then?

A father sat at the breakfast table with his recently graduated son. The young man had been a recognized leader in his high school. During school years, he had seemed relaxed and confident. As the father looked at his son, it appeared to him that he had become much more serious overnight. He almost seemed to have shrunk. The father reached over and put a reassuring arm on his son's shoulder. "It's a big world out there, isn't it?" he said, echoing the young man's unspoken fears.

Indeed it is. One moves from the top of one's organization to the bottom. There is no clear prescription for what to do next.

From a broad perspective, the new high school graduate has three basic options from which to choose: (a) go to work full-time—if a job is available; (b) train for a career while working (apprenticeships, military service, and on-the-job training are all possibilities); or (c) go for more schooling (four-year colleges, two-year junior and community colleges, business, trade, vocational, or technical schools are all possibilities).

Luther Otto points out there are two labor-force realities to consider in sorting out which of these paths to follow. The realities are:

- The vast majority of occupations require additional training or education beyond high school.

- Many employers hire on the basis of the applicant's credentials. Therefore additional education or specialized training opens up more and better occupational opportunities.[7]

Senior-high students and their parents need to investigate those options so they can make a wise decision about next steps. Let's look at each of the three choices.

Employment

One can go directly to full-time work after high school. Normally, this does seem to limit one's chances for the future, particularly in our high-tech age. However, there are persons for whom this might be a good choice. A few might find a job that will develop and train them as they go. Some are tired of school and do not feel ready yet to face more years of schooling. Others may be a bit late maturing. They may not feel ready to leave home for the type of schooling they may eventually want to explore. Others may feel so undecided about why go to college and what to pursue at college that a postponement seems fitting.

It is important for such persons not to feel they have made a once-and-for-all decision. Educational institutions are increasingly becoming places for persons of all ages. There will be opportunity to elect some advanced education at a later time, if the student so chooses.

We are aware of a young man who, after having trouble with studies in high school decided to join the navy. This dismayed his parents, who were strong believers in education. In the course of his experience as an enlisted man, he became aware of how difficult a time his married friends were having living on enlisted pay. When he finished his term of service, he decided he should try a little more education—first junior college and then a four-year school. He is now successfully employed, providing well for his family.

Training While Working

One can train for a career while working. Night school, military service, on-the-job training, and apprenticeships offer this sort of opportunity. Of these, apprenticeships may well offer some young adults the greatest access to many skilled and satisfying occupations.

What is apprenticeship? It is the combination of work and training in an authorized program to prepare a limited number of persons to be qualified in a field of work. There are more than three-hundred apprentice-learned trades in the United States. They include airplane or automobile mechanic, barber, blacksmith, boiler maker, cabinet maker, carpenter, chef, electroplater, and engraver. Many of these are highly competitive and admit only a few persons a year. Many will not admit a person until two or more years after high school.

How can a young person enter one of the apprentice trades? Charlotte Lobb notes five routes that young people have successfully taken to become apprentices:

1. *Connections.* One finds a relative or friend in the trade and has them suggest one's name when openings occur.
2. *Testing.* Some programs have formalized testing procedures that are offered infrequently. It is well to keep frequent contact so one will not miss the opportunity to be considered through testing.
3. *School.* Whether or not courses are a formal part of an apprenticeship program, taking courses in the field in which one has interest may open up opportunities.
4. *Tenacity.* Bill applied at the same plumbing shop six times in eighteen months before he was hired. Reapplying at the same shops every two or three months is acceptable.
5. *Starting at a lower job.* Begin to work at whatever entry level job is available in a company that has the trade one wants to pursue. This has opened the door into apprenticeship for many persons.[8]

College or University

Many new high school graduates will be planning to go on to college. For an increasing number, this will be the right decision. Recently, the Hudson Institute indicated there will be higher educational requirements for the new jobs created in the next ten years. Higher levels of math, language, and reasoning skills will be required.

The number of jobs in the least-skilled areas will decrease, and those in the high-skilled professions will increase. Today 22 percent of all occupations require a college degree. Almost a third of the new jobs created in the next decades will be filled by college graduates.

The jobs that require a college degree are frequently the ones that offer the highest salaries. It is now estimated that a person under thirty with a college degree will earn four times as much money as someone without one. (Twenty years ago, the difference was only twice as great.)

Deciding whether to go to college, selecting a college, and preparing for it—including making financial plans—are critical tasks. We will provide some guidance for this in the closing section of this chapter.

BASIC ISSUES

Meanwhile, adolescents and their families are experiencing pressing day-to-day issues. Repeatedly, families face concerns with their youths that may appear to be removed from vocational discovery and development. In truth, however, each of these matters is important for the youths' unfolding career discoveries. Let's take a look at some of these issues.

Freedom

"What time do I have to be home?" The key issue here is "How much freedom, when?" In this period, people change physically from children to near adults. Naturally, they also want to change from a child's condition—having adults make their decisions for them—to adult autonomy. Parents and teenage children may have many battles about how quickly one may gain freedom to make one's own decisions. They may differ over the areas in which the young person may have freedom.

Quite likely, the eighteen-year-old will have many freedoms and decisions. This will be true whether the choice is to attend college, find employment away from home, or enter military service. The eighteen-year-old will be able to decide what to wear, eat, drink; when to go to bed and when to get up; how much to sleep, work, study, attend class, recreate; and more.

Some who are thrust in this environment are so unused to such freedom that they are overwhelmed and blow it. Others have been experiencing a greater degree of responsibility and freedom throughout their adolescent years. They feel ready for the decisions they will face as young adults living independently. Wise is the family that has balanced the freedom/responsibility issue over the adolescent years so the young adult is ready for it.

School Issues

"What courses shall I take? How hard should I study? What's most important?" Though some of the more detailed career decisions are years away, youths and their families need to act on some hunches as to those future decisions. They will do this in course selection during middle and senior high school. Does the person anticipate a college experience, a particular vocation? These issues may be first explored in school years. Such course selections involve awareness of the future importance of present choices.

There are some cautions to observe. If a student is still having reading difficulties, these should be addressed. (It is estimated that about 13 percent of all seventeen-year-olds are functionally illiterate.) Also, the basic math skills that may be required for any possible work interests should be mastered. Far too many persons who choose college find themselves having to take remedial reading, English, or math classes.

Some educators note an increase in the number of students avoiding the vocational or college-preparation classes in favor of less-demanding general classes. They point out that such programs prepare students for neither work nor further education.

Course selection, amount of attention given to studies, and corrective steps for any earlier educational gaps are important issues to face now. Failure to do so may close doors or cause delays in realizing future hopes and plans.

Automobile

May I use the family car? May I have a car of my own? Many parents have experienced the good news/bad news phenomenon when their children obtain their drivers' licenses. The good news is that the young people no longer need to be chauffeured to all of their activities—they can drive themselves. The may even be willing to deliver brothers and sisters and run errands, just for the joy of driving. Bad news includes higher auto insurance rates and the decreased availability of the family car. (As an old joke puts it, "What do you call the parents of teenage drivers? Pedestrians!")

The question may arise, "Wouldn't it be easier if I had my own car? That way, we wouldn't have all these scheduling hassles!"

There are at least two issues at stake here. One is the matter of family financial resources and the use of those resources. Before answering about the car, a family may want to explore what projected post-high school education is likely to cost. They will also want to explore together what a car would cost—buying it, taxes, license, insurance, maintenance, repair, gas, oil, replacement. If the family does not have enough resources for both, it would be tragic to buy the car and give up on the education.

Still another issue has to do with *short-term versus long-term gratifications.* What luxuries would parents like their adolescent children to experience now? What particular pleasures do they ask them to postpone—and perhaps have the joy of earning for themselves?

Two parents with whom we visited faced this issue with each of their three children. They concluded that they did not have enough money both to provide children's cars and to help provide education for them. These parents said yes to the education but no to the car. It was inconvenient but not impossible for their children to attend their respective universities without a car. The parents made exceptions when two daughters needed cars during their senior years to do required field education placements. For the other, help in obtaining a car was part of a college graduation present.

Speaking of costly investments, it may be more important to arrive at college with a personal computer (and the ability to use it) than with a car. At one college, 75 percent of all students own personal computers!

Part-Time Employment

Still another question is, "Shall I get a job? If so, what kind?" Two kinds of jobs are possible. One is the volunteer opportunity. A wide variety of groups, organizations, and agencies seek volunteer assistance and include teenagers among those they recruit. Charlotte Lobb has described how valuable this may be for them. The benefits lie both in the service rendered and in the self-discoveries they may make (and the mistakes they may avoid). For example, she tells of Mike, who thought he wanted to be a doctor. And so as a high school junior, he volunteered ten hours a week at a general hospital, lending a hand in several departments. While he enjoyed it all, he found himself increasingly requesting assignment in the physical therapy department. He was fascinated by the work of helping disabled children learn to walk again, paraplegics struggle to be able to stand again, and stroke victims regain the use of their arms. Out of his volunteer activity, Mike discovered that he wanted very much to be a physical therapist. He realized that although the eventual income would not be as high as that of a physician, the personal rewards for him would be greater. By contrast, she tells of Maria, who had always been told she would be a good teacher. And so she took the educational preparation for it. Not until she had finished three years of college was she faced with a real teaching situation, and she hated it! Had she spent some time as a volunteer—a teacher's aide, tutor, camp counselor, or recreation leader—she might have had a more realistic idea of what teaching really entailed. She might have been spared that false start. There are a wide variety of careers one can explore through volunteerism.[9]

The other jobs are those that offer pay. They may provide some of the same advantages of self-discovery. Fast-food restaurants and retail stores employ large numbers of young people. A paying job may be valued for many reasons: prestige, companionship, independence. It may well provide an opportunity for one to discover one's self-management skills (punctuality, dependability, etc.) and to develop new ones. However, the big attraction is the pay. Increased finances for what the teenager wants may be the drawing card to the job. This in turn raises other issues in the family: Whose is the income from the teenager's job? the teenager's own to use as one wishes? the teenager's own, but to be used with parental guidance? the family's? Is some to be saved for the future, including for college if the student chooses?

Jobs during school do have some drawbacks. Work hours will include evenings and weekends and may not be very flexible. This may invade study time or school and church group activities. With any job, a youth and his or her family may want to explore the questions: Can this be kept within reasonable time limits? What will be the gains? the losses? In this rushed period of my life, what do I most want to do with my time?

Sex and Sexuality

There is another question: "What about sex and sexuality?" This may well be the unspoken question in many homes. Both adults and their adolescent children sometimes find it difficult to speak about this vital topic with each other. However, dialogue is needed for many reasons. In our limited space, we will speak only of the occupational reasons.

It is now estimated by the U.S. Centers for Disease Control that 51.5 percent of females aged fifteen to nineteen have engaged in premarital sex, compared to 29 percent in 1970. The biggest increase is among younger teenagers. In 1970, less than 5 percent of fifteen-year-old females had had sexual intercourse. By the 1990s this had increased to 26 percent of females and 33 percent of males of this age. The percentage of eighteen-year-old females who had had intercourse rose from 39 percent (in 1970) to 69 percent at this writing.[10] The average age for first intercourse among American teenagers is 16.2 for girls and 15.7 for boys.

Beside those statistics, let us place another one. It is estimated that of 100 couples who are having intercourse regularly (without birth control), 85 will conceive within a year. The likelihood of pregnancy for sexually active youths is very high. The consequences of such a pregnancies can be tragic from many points of view, including their occupational life chances. Arthur A. Campbell once wrote:

> The timing of the first birth is of crucial strategic importance in the lives of young women, because the need to take care of a baby limits severely their ability to take advantage of opportunities that might have changed their lives for the better. In this regard, the problems posed by births to unmarried women are especially serious. The girl who has an illegitimate child at the age of 16 has 90 percent of her life's script written for her. She will probably drop out of school; even if someone else in her

family helps to take care of the baby, she will probably not be able to find a steady job that pays enough to provide for herself and her child; she may feel impelled to marry someone she might not otherwise have chosen. Her life choices are few, and most of them are bad. Had she been able to delay the first child, her prospects might have been quite different, assuming that she would have had opportunities to continue her education, improve her vocational skills, find a job, marry someone she wanted to marry, and have a child when she and her husband were ready for it. Also, the child would have been born under quite different circumstances and might grow up in a stable family environment.[11]

While Campbell spoke of the young woman, many of the same things could be said about the young man. Increasingly, young men are rightfully being held accountable for pregnancies. Therefore a similar limitation of their life chances may result from an unwanted pregnancy.

Sadly, all too many teenagers are caught in this dilemma. The birth rates for white teenagers in the United States are higher than those for teenagers in any other western country (and the rate for African American teenagers is three times as high). Proportionately, U.S. teenagers under eighteen have twice as many babies as British and Canadian teens, more than three times as many as the French, and more than four times as many as the Swedish and the Dutch.[12]

Of course, the time to talk about sexuality and values is long before adolescence. Whether or not the topic has been discussed previously, it is important that parents communicate their own values, feelings, and beliefs about sex and sexuality. And yet, they cannot ignore that their children may be deeply involved in a peer culture whose values are quite different.

Parents will want to offer guidance concerning their children's sexual decisions. However, parents may feel the need to add that if children choose not to follow their lead, they must at least take precautions to decrease the chance that an unwanted pregnancy occurs. They may want to be sure that youths have access to reliable information. Exposure to the AIDS virus can lead to tragedy. Unwanted teenage pregnancies place serious burdens on the young parents, their families, and the conceived child. Such pregnancies may bring pain to the persons involved and will almost certainly decrease their available life chances and range of occupational choices.

Faith

The parents may be wondering, "What about faith and vocational awareness during these years?" These are vital years in which the youth may appear to be forsaking or seriously questioning their faith.

It might be helpful to speak of the insights of John Westerhoff. A theologian and educator, Westerhoff suggests that persons pass through four stages of faith, which he compares to the growth of a tree. At any stage, the tree is whole and complete—it simply adds rings of growth as it ages and matures. Westerhoff suggests the four stages are:

1. *Experienced faith:* the faith of childhood. One explores, imagines, creates, imitates, experiences, has fun, wonders, experiences hugs and caresses. Questions of faith and doctrine are not important. Great experiences are.
2. *Affiliative faith:* the faith of belonging of being in community. In this stage there is a rich sense of being a part of something important, the dominance of religious affections, giving the group or organization a great sense of authority.
3. *Searching faith:* faith expressed through searching, doubt, critical judgment. There is the need to experiment with other beliefs and lifestyles. Westerhoff comments, "In order to move from an understanding of faith that belongs to the community to an understanding of faith that is our own, we need to count and question that faith."[13]
4. *Owned faith:* faith as a central part of one's being. Though there are still questions, one is willing to stand on what one believes and wants to put it into personal and social action.[14]

In the adolescent years, a person may be in either the "affiliative faith" or the "searching faith" stage, in both at the same time, or bouncing back from one to the other. The questioning, doubting, abandoning, may be hard to take. However, this is part of the faith journey. This faith adventure will likely continue into the post-high school years. At their best, parents will need to trust the process. This means giving some freedom on these matters while living, sharing, and inviting from their own faith perspective. This faith searching has a parallel in one's vocational searching. Is there a Divine element in my choice of occupation and career or is it all up to me?

WHAT PARENTS OF ADOLESCENTS CAN DO

Question: This is all very interesting. But as parent am I not "out of it" (in more ways than one) by now? Hasn't my adolescent child and his or her teachers and guidance counselors taken over this task?

Answer: You should not be out of this process even though most of us parents feel that way at times. Actually, your child may be receiving less guidance than you think. Most high school guidance offices only respond to the young person who takes the initiative (unless the person is experiencing some sort of difficulty). The young person may be muddling through some difficult decisions without talking to any knowledgeable adult about them. Parents and school officials are sometimes left out. Young people may discuss their options only with peers, who may not be knowledgeable about all these choices.

Question: That's just it! Throughout this chapter you have spoken of the importance of the youth's gaining acceptance with the peer group. My child's friends have become the confidants, the counselors, the consultants about my child's present and future decisions—not me!

Answer: Don't give up so easily. Peers—individually and in groups —are very influential. However, so are the parents who enter into this process.

Peers will probably have strong influence about clothing, hair, music, fashions, fads. Yet the parents who stay in conversation with their teenage children have an important voice in many crucial matters. Dr. John Hill, chair of the psychology department at Virginia Commonwealth University, has summarized the research about parent-youth issues:

- In most cases young people continue to have a very positive emotional relationship with their parents.

- There is no evidence for widespread disillusionment over parent-child ties during the adolescent period.

- The way emotion and affection are expressed by young people changes, just as it changes from infancy to early childhood.

- In matters of basic values, including religion and political beliefs, there is as much difference among adolescents and their peer group, as there is between adolescents and their parents.

- When young people set educational and occupational goals, parents are more influential than adolescent friends, high school teachers, counselors, or any other group.[15]

Dr. Luther Otto and associates have carried on an intensive study of approximately seven thousand young adults in the ten to fifteen years after high school. Overwhelmingly, he discovered two responses: (a) they would like more help in discovering and adjusting to a career and (b) one of the sources from which they would like more help is their own parents. One young adult's comment is typical of many others. "Maybe this is passing the buck, but I think my parents left my future pretty much up to me. . . . A little more guidance or direction would have helped me to define a better future for myself."[16]

It is important to open the door of conversation with adolescents about post-high school plans. It is also vital to keep the dialogue going over the next several years.

Question: If I am to still be involved, I suspect my style with my children will have to change from the all-knowing authority that it once was. Am I correct?

Answer: You certainly are. Your style changed from your children's infancy, to their early childhood, to their later childhood. A new way of relating is now needed.

Both you and your child hope that in the fairly near future she or he will be independent, competent, successful. You will both want to deal with each other in a way that leads to that destination. That means very few or no ultimatums. It means listening, hearing, offering suggestions, brainstorming, mutually investigating, exchanging information. It means frank revelation and discussion about your income and family resources. You will need to negotiate how much of those resources you are willing to invest in your child's education. It may be how much you can afford, or it may be what you feel is wise.

Question: This sounds both exciting and complicated! I haven't done much of this with my child, and time's a-wasting! How do I start?

Answer: You might start by rereading this chapter and making a list of the topics that you'd like to discuss with your adolescent child. Then go out together for a soft drink or a meal and talk a little about it. (Be brief—long parental speeches always turn children off.) Invite your child to express thoughts and ideas. Listen with acceptance. Ask questions. Look for points of agreement. Try to locate points of disagreement and explore ways to build bridges across those.

Don't be discouraged if it doesn't go too far the first time. Keep trying. You may not even know how you are doing. However, this is a topic that won't go away. There will be more opportunities.

Go to it. Good luck and God bless!

Question: My daughter and I have additional difficulties in all this. You have spoken of flexible gender roles and of helping school fit the needs of the student.

My daughter has great interest and ability in math and science. I feel she has promise in some engineering or related field. However, she doesn't feel encouraged in these interests at her school. Rather she feels strange, neglected, ignored, sometimes harassed in these classes. Do you think she is imagining things?

Answer: Probably not. Recently, the respected American Association of University Women (AAUW) issued the results of a study on this topic. They entitled it *How Schools Shortchange Girls.* Their research revealed a number of disturbing discoveries. For example, they found that on the average, girls receive less attention from classroom teachers than do boys. Also, sexual harassment of girls by boys—from innuendo to assault—is increasing. This is often particularly true when a girl enters a male-dominated field, like engineering or construction.

They discovered that the difference between girls and boys in math achievement is small and declining. However, the gender gap in science is not decreasing. For some reason, girls who are highly competent in math and science are less likely to elect advanced classes or technological careers than are their male classmates. Too often, girls seem to experience a drop in both math confidence and achievement in the middle-school years. The drop in confidence preceded the decline in achievement. The study suggested that high-achieving girls are not given as much encouragement to pursue scientific careers as boys.[17]

Question: Is there anything I can do, as a parent, on my daughter's behalf?

Answer: Yes, there are at least three things.

First, you can examine your own attitudes and practices as a parent. Psychologist Jacquelynne Eccles (who has studied for years the development of science and math interest in students) finds that parents still have different approaches to daughters than to sons. They may send different messages to sons and daughters. A boy's success in science may be attributed to natural ability, a girl's to hard work. A stereotype may prevail that science is less important and more difficult for girls. The most important influence is a student's self-perception and that of parents and teachers. Parents may give gifts to perpetuate the stereotypes. When the children are younger, boys may get building blocks and chemistry sets while girls receive Barbie dolls.[18] Begin by looking at yourself.

Second, parents can advocate for a more open school system. They can obtain a copy of the AAUW report we mentioned and discuss it with teachers, administrators, and school boards.

Third, parents can help their daughters find support systems within their chosen field. At present, engineering may be a lonely career choice; only 4 percent of engineers today are women. Still, they can be introduced to persons in the field. They can be helped to find a university that has women professors on the faculty. Some schools are creating support groups for women in science. Every bit of support helps.

Question: In all that has been discussed in this chapter, I think I missed something. What, specifically, are my parental opportunities to offer a faith vision of vocation when my child is in the adolescent years?

Answer: There are many opportunities. Youths' great desire for intimacy and peer group acceptance is a hunger for what the Bible calls *koinonia.* Translated as "fellowship" or "communion," the word describes communal feeling between a person and God and among people. A group of people—or one person—can help an individual experience God's love. This connects to that faith of belonging of which we spoke. Wise and fortunate are the parents who are able to offer the options of wholesome friends and groups. These may come from church and family friends.

Still another part is adolescents' growing ability to reason, question, doubt, and search. They may apply these skills to their faith and come into the searching faith stage. Parental acceptance, encouragement, participation, dialogue during this searching phase (now and later) will be a valuable contribution.

Decisions about what to do with money the youth has earned is another opportunity. You can communicate that part of your vocation is the way you use your money—spending, saving, giving, and thus being involved in needs and causes beyond your immediate circle.

As your adolescent sorts out post-high school opportunities, you will want for him or her the very best. That willing the very best is the starting place for Christian vocation—to become, as the ad puts it, "all that you can be." Your willingness to sacrifice to make this possible and encouraging your child to be responsible are valuable expressions of the Christian concept of stewardship, which simply means managing all we are and have before God.

The possibilities are many! They are implicit in the important decisions your adolescent child and you are facing together.

Questions and Answers for Parents of the College-Bound

Question: If my child and I agree that college is the right decision, then what? How do we decide which college or university?

Answer: That's an even more complex question than you might realize. In the United States, there are three thousand degree-granting institutions and another ten thousand that award certificates. Colleges come in many shapes, sizes, and kinds. People need a way to sort through these many possibilities without getting bogged down in confusion.

Fortunately, there is a way to accomplish that sorting out. Much of the needed information is provided in condensed form in a number of books, available at public libraries or school career centers. One of the best of these is *The College Handbook.* Other good sources are *Barron's Profiles of American Colleges, Chronicle Four-Year College Data Book, College Planning/Search Book, Lovejoy's College Guide,* and *Peterson's Annual Guide to Undergraduate Study.*

A student and parent should prepare a list of questions about each college or university that holds a possible interest. Some questions might be:

- Is this a school that I would find comfortable in terms of size, geographical location, type of community in which it is located, and racial/ethnic composition?

- Does it appear I could be admitted there? Would I be bored? in over my head?

- Does it offer fields that hold a possible interest for me?

- Is it affordable? How much does it cost, and what kind of financial aid is available?

Of course each person will also have additional questions. Spending time developing one's own questions and gaining some preliminary answers from college guides is a good start.

Question: Then what? How soon do we need to start?

Answer: Luther Otto suggests the following timetable for college planning:

1. *Junior year, fall semester:* The family should begin talking with their son or daughter about what he or she wants from a college experience. The first ten pages in *The College Handbook* might be a good discussion opener. Also, begin to talk about financing a college education.

2. *Junior year, spring semester:* It is time to get serious about identifying colleges that match some of the student's interests. It will be good to attend college fairs and talk with college representatives. Discover what admissions tests (the SAT or the ACT) the colleges of interest require. Arrange to take those tests.

3. *Junior year, summer:* Encourage your son or daughter to write to colleges of interest for catalogs, financial aid information, and an application. Invite persons who attend colleges under consideration—persons who may be home for the summer. Together, you can visit with that student about his or her college.

4. *Senior year, fall semester:* Encourage your son or daughter to pay attention to financial aid announcements. Are there deadlines that should be noted?

Take college admissions tests if that has not been done.

Narrow colleges to a manageable number, and if possible, visit some of them. (See the appendix to this book, "How to Visit a College Campus.") It is best to do so on weekdays when students are on campus, classes are in session, and administrative offices are open. Add to your impressions and evaluation of each school.

Apply to and request financial aid from the schools in which you are interested. We emphasize that it is important to apply both for admission and financial aid in the fall, or by January at the latest. Very probably all financial aid will be awarded by spring.

5. *Senior year, spring semester:* Encourage your son or daughter to continue checking on a weekly basis for scholarship and financial aid announcements. Complete financial aid application forms. (Often these are based on your federal income tax form, so you may need to do your income tax early.) Celebrate the acceptances from colleges or universities that your son or daughter receives. Shrug off the nonacceptances. After all, one can only go to one place at a time. Make a choice.[19]

Question: While I want my child to go to college, I am worried about finances. How can I anticipate expenses? Will there be financial aid available?

Answer: A good place to start is with two helpful booklets, often found in high school guidance centers: "Applying for Financial Aid" and "Meeting College Costs." The College Scholarship Service of the College Board also provides an early financial aid planning service that might provide a realistic preview as to what can be expected. The family also needs to discuss what part of the financing is the parents' responsibility and what part is the student's.

What can one expect as regards financial aid? The amount of aid varies from year to year and decade to decade. Still, some basic principles seem to guide institutions' determination of how to award financial aid. First, it is assumed that the family, together with the student, bears primary responsibility for meeting college education costs. Within the family's ability to pay, it is expected to do so. While there are some merit financial aid awards, based on high grades or achievement in some area (usually sports), these are a small part of financial aid today. Most of it is awarded on a determination of family need.

Second, financial aid is intended to meet estimated need. The student's family supplies information about income, savings, assets, debts, liabilities, size of family, number of persons in college. A formula is then applied to estimate what the family and student can pay toward the costs of attending a particular institution.

Third, financial aid is given in a "package concept." The total aid given any student consists of a combination of three parts: (a) "gift aid"—scholarships and grants that do not need to be repaid; (b) loans, which do have to be repaid; and (c) work grants, which involve obligations on the part of the student. The loans will be at an attractive rate and be payable over several years after the student graduates from or leaves the college.

An Associated Press article pointed out six myths that create confusion about college costs.

Myth 1: "It doesn't pay to save for college costs." The faulty assumption is that if a family doesn't have savings, the college will it rescue with financial aid. The truth is that while savings are figured in the formula for financial aid, the formula weighs income more heavily than assets and savings in calculating the family's contribution.

Myth 2: "The higher the tuition, the better the school." This is not necessarily true. Many schools provide excellent education at relatively modest cost.

Myth 3: "Federal student aid has plunged in the 1980s and 1990s." Actually, government and other aid has been decreasing for a longer period than that. The biggest change is that from the 1970s to the 1990s the amount of student aid in the form of loans grew from one-fifth to one-half. Students and their families are assuming more college debts than previously.

Myth 4: "I can't afford the most selective and costly schools." The truth is that it is wise to apply to every school that interests one and request financial aid. Many have scholarship programs that make it affordable for more than one might imagine.

Myth 5: "Why bother applying for financial aid? I probably don't qualify." This is not necessarily true. The number of children in college, the cost of the college, and several other factors may make persons eligible. You have nothing to lose by applying and finding out.

Myth 6: "You can work your way through school." Actually, most summer jobs and student employment during the year pay only the minimum wage. A student who works twelve hours a week (which is the average), at minimum wage, can expect to earn 6 percent of an annual college bill.[20] Students and their parents need to gather accurate information to make wise financial decisions about education.

Having said all that, we have not told you—because we cannot— what amount of financial aid your son or daughter will receive. Filing applications early, providing all necessary data, and carefully following instructions will give you both the best chance and the most complete information.

7

Moving into Adulthood: From Eighteen to Thirty

Parents of young adults have learned something that other parents do not yet know. They know that parenting never ends—only the roles and the rules change!

During these years, your son or daughter completes the transition from childhood to adulthood, moving from preparation to the world of work. Let's take a closer look.

LATER ADOLESCENCE—FROM EIGHTEEN TO TWENTY-TWO

Initiation to Adulthood

When Daniel Levinson and associates did their pioneering research on adult life stages, they drew some fascinating conclusions. They discovered that a person's life evolves through a series of overlapping eras, each of them about twenty-five years in duration. They see the four eras of life as these:

1. *Childhood and adolescence:* birth to age twenty-two.
2. *Early adulthood:* age seventeen to forty-five.
3. *Middle adulthood:* age forty to sixty-five.
4. *Late adulthood:* age sixty to death.

These researchers note that each era has its own distinctive and unifying qualities. That is, each era is rather like the act of a play or the major section of a novel.

On the border between each of these stages, there is a "zone of overlap." That is the period when the old era is being completed and the new one is starting. This is not a simple, brief transition. It is rather the change of the fabric of one's life. Such transitions take four or five years. One's task in this time is to link the eras of one's life and provide some continuity between them.

The first of these sensitive, delicate, zones of overlap occurs in the years seventeen to twenty-two. This is the early adult transition. (The next zones of overlap will occur at age forty to forty-five—the middle adult transition; and at age sixty to sixty-five—the late adult transition.)[1]

The period from ages seventeen to twenty-two is a significant transitional time. It has some of the same emotion, difficulty, and trauma as one's midlife transition! One enters this era a child-becoming-an-adult. One leaves this era with decisions and preparations to be a self-sufficient adult.

During these years, it is quite normal to have some confusion, frustration, and quite possibly a few false starts. Young adults may need to learn to be patient with themselves. Parents may need to discover patience with them. The young adult who discovers that he or she is in a career track that doesn't feel right is wise to escape.

Developmental Tasks

So far we have been have been looking at years from eighteen to twenty-two as the initiation into adulthood. Now, let's look at those same years from a slightly different viewpoint—as continuing the growth of childhood and adolescence.

From this point of view, this era has yet other developmental tasks. One of these is achieving independence from one's parents. Many skills learned earlier prepare a person for this step. Dressing oneself, managing money, cooking, driving a car, reading, writing—these and other skills equip a person for independent living.

Many persons will express this autonomy by moving out of the parental home. (However, many are finding it necessary to stay home longer or return home. Autonomy feels different when the young adult must remain home.) The move may be to college, to military service, to employment in another community, or to a room or apartment. Both parent and child will probably have mixed feelings about this step.

They understand that it is necessary, and yet both may resist it at times. Most frequently, though, the youth eagerly seeks autonomy and the parents find themselves resisting. Once young people have achieved autonomy, then they are often ready to reestablish a mutually meaningful relationship with their family. Some young adults may work on this issue while still living at home.

Though the struggle for autonomy is a reasonable step, it often does not feel that way within the family. A person may reject family faith, religion, values, practices, and more. Even though parents have given a firm foundation, the eighteen- to twenty-two-year-old seeks that which he or she independently chooses. This may involve saying no to some well-loved family beliefs. It may take a few more years to be ready to say yes once again to parents' faith and values.

Another developmental task is rethinking or clarifying one's gender identity. This has been developing through the years. Same-sex and opposite-sex friendships, peer groups, dating and other relationships, and bodily and hormonal changes have contributed to this development. In the late adolescent years, it is expected that the person will be capable of fulfilling an effective gender role that ideally includes becoming capable of sexual intimacy. There is much variety as to how flexible persons understand these gender roles to be. This in turn has important implications for career discovery.

Still another task is the continued development of an internal morality. Young adults begin to discover that there are many moral values. Therefore they need to distinguish between basic values and secondary values. Furthermore, individuals at this stage may face a wider range of challenges to their values. These challenges may require ethical decisions that the person has not faced before. Someone may ask permission to copy a paper the student has written. A young adult may need to decide about spending the weekend with another person when sexual intimacy may be expected. It may be necessary to decide whether to engage in political or campus protests. Questions may arise whether to maintain one's religious heritage or to rethink it.

Each of these decisions will need to be made in the light of the individual's own internalized set of moral principles and values. One must sort out one's received moral teachings, one's personally chosen moral ideals, and the nature of the circumstances one is facing. Out of these, one's set of values arises.[2]

Moral questions are not easy questions. They are particularly troubling for the late adolescent, who at the same time is struggling for the right to ask them! This, again, is a parental opportunity to communicate about vocation. Giving your son or daughter permission and encouragement to work on moral reasoning is a gift. Mutual dialogue (without dominating or being dogmatic) about moral reasoning is a further gift.

Another developmental task is that of career choice. We will look at this in more detail below. For the moment, we will simply note that career choice is an expression of one's value system and one's self-understanding. Therefore, it is wise to take time to know oneself as clearly as possible before making a strong commitment to a particular career. Of course, tentative choices need to be stated and investigated. The search for autonomy may involve rejecting models (including parental models) and values that one may later embrace. We think of dozens of persons who once stated that they would *never* pursue their parents' careers. Later on, they elected to do just that!

Some research should be mentioned here. This research concerned persons who had chosen to enter theological school at a later point in life—as a second career. In interviews, many of these persons revealed that although they had been drawn to religious vocations in college, they did not heed that inner urging at that time, for one reason or another. Later, they began to pursue that to which they had felt drawn earlier in their lives. This may well be true of other occupations as well. If so, it would be wise to counsel, "Listen to your heart. Listen to your inner urging and your inner directions. Are there stirrings within you that may be part of your leading? If so, you will be happier if you are in tune with those inner persuasions." Both external information and inner leadings are important in discovering one's vocation.

The central issue is *individual identity versus role diffusion*. What about me is most important to those who hold significance for me? In what ways do I express my family identity and in what ways do I dissociate from it? What are the cultural expectations of me? the societal expectations? What do I make of these—do I accept and fulfill them, or do I reject and rebel against them? How do I integrate all the roles I play into a personal identity—family member, student, citizen, worker, believer, friend, sexual being, and more?

There are many possible pitfalls around this issue. First, one may be assigned a *negative identity*. Phrases such as "failure, good-for-nothing, juvenile delinquent, hood, greaser" may be applied to an individual during a period of experimentation. A person may be called "clumsy, stupid, lazy," by someone in authority. The person may accept this identity and continue to behave in ways that will strengthen it.

A second pitfall is *identity foreclosure*—that is, making decisions about one's identity too soon and not growing and investigating any further. This may happen to those who marry too young and/or become parents in early adulthood. However, it is by no means limited to them. Others may decide in childhood or early adolescence that they will become what their parents or grandparents want them to be. They imitate these roles without personal reflection and growth.

A third pitfall is *role diffusion,* in which young people may feel unable to commit to a single unified view of themselves or to integrate their various roles. Such an individual may have difficulty choosing between conflicting values and may lack confidence to make meaningful decisions. For some time, the eighteen- to twenty-two-year-old may have feelings of anxiety, apathy, and possibly anger.

There may be times of confusion and depression. After all, a person is attempting to bring together all the elements of his or her experience into a coordinated self-understanding. Feelings of isolation, self-preoccupation, and discouragement may quite normally be experienced.[3]

We should also anticipate a good deal of role experimentation at this stage. Indeed, this is the central process for working through the identity issue. This experimentation may include trying a variety of jobs, changing college majors, transferring from college to college, doing extensive daydreaming. It may also include dating a wide variety of persons or evaluating one's commitment to one's religion. Further, it might involve investigating other religions and value systems or being active in new choices of political parties or action groups. The person in this stage may want to wander and travel a good bit. Erik Erikson has described this time as a "moratorium." By this, he means a period of free experimentation before a reasonably firm identity is achieved.[4]

Career Decisions

As a part of this search, late adolescents will make some career decisions. They have several career tasks in these years. As we noted, one of these is crystallization (tentative, preliminary choice of a general field of work). Another is specification of a possible career within that general area. And yet another is implementation, which involves completing training and gaining an entry position.

The Late Adolescent at College

Many will participate in this growing process on a college campus. Experiences on campus may aid a growing sense of self and some initiation into a career. We will first reflect on this college experience from the broad perspective of its contribution to self-discovery. Then we will look at campus life as a place for career discovery.

Self-Discovery on Campus: Probably the biggest decision the eighteen-year-old has made is "What will I do after high school? If I choose college, which college will I attend?" Now the young person faces the biggest task he or she has ever faced, "How do I survive in this place where I said I wanted to go?" The new student lives with many transitions, including a sense of dislocation and loss. At the same time, he or she also asks, "Who am I, apart from my family, my church, my school?"[5]

Coburn and Treeger offer the following thoughts as to what it is like to be a brand-new freshman coming to a university:

> You are leaving behind everyone you know and moving to a new place where you have made a commitment to spend the next four years. . . .
>
> When you arrive in this strange place, you look around and see a landscape of unfamiliar faces. . . . They all look smart, confident, and outgoing.
>
> No one here knows anything about the status you had in your previous position—or about any of your past accomplishments.
>
> You have left behind your family, friends, colleagues—all the people who are important in your life.
>
> You're not too sure where anything is or who might be able to help you.

You have to share a small room with a perfect stranger. There are no set guidelines about bedtime, use of the phone, stereo, radio, or entertaining guests. You have to negotiate everything.

You have more work to do than ever before, but you're not too sure how you will be evaluated or what people want from you. You may not get your first evaluations for many weeks.

You have a lot of unscheduled time and there are plenty of distractions. . . .

You have to handle financial and housekeeping matters that used to be done for you or, at least, you shared.

You're not too sure where your work and new relationships are heading, and you don't know where or how you will ever fit into this new place. But everyone has told you that your whole future depends on your doing well during these four years—preferably better than those other bright, confident-looking people who live here with you.[6]

There is much more going on in the freshman year of college than academics, although academic performance is important. (Too little performance costs one the privilege of staying!) The college experience is about separation from family and home, about discovering and maintaining oneself in a strange environment. It is about learning to live with a roommate. An important part is discovering how to handle freedom and responsibility. It is learning to make friends in a new setting and finding one's place within that setting. As Mary Ackerman, dean of students at Macalaster College, notes, "It's about the question 'Who am I?' and 'How do I fit in?'"[7]

There are related but distinct issues for students living at home while attending college. Although the same issues of self-discovery apply, students who commute must also learn to balance additional demands on their time, including travel to and from classes, part-time or full-time employment, and being a member of a household.

As students discover that they can survive and develop some new understandings of themselves, other issues will arise. Many students speak of a "sophomore slump," coming sometime after they have survived that first strangeness. One student recalls:

I felt like the character in the *Roadrunner* cartoon—you know, running frantically full speed ahead, straight off of a cliff—and that awful moment when he looks down and realizes there's no ground under him— that he's just out there by himself in the middle of the air. That's how I felt most of my sophomore year.[8]

Similarly, another student recollects:

My sophomore year was a very tenuous time for me. I was very frightened. I was afraid I was drifting apart from my friends at home. I wasn't quite sure where I was going, what direction. I had no solid ground to pin myself to intellectually. I was aware of time flying by. Tuition was going up each year. What did I have to show for it?[9]

Many sophomores, juniors, and seniors find themselves overwhelmed by the freedom and the choices. There are endless choices of courses, majors, friends, activities, politics, religion, and lifestyles. They can elect to transfer, interrupt their education for a time, or even study abroad. However, they are becoming acutely aware that to choose one thing is to give up another.

The choice of a major field of study may be one of the more stressful choices during a college education. While some students may come to college fully aware of their gifts and what major to pursue, they are in the minority. Some studies indicate that this group may comprise only 10 to 15 percent of the student population.

Some who arrive knowing, discover they don't know after all. Persons who want to pursue premedical or some other preprofessional studies may discover that they need to give up that dream. For a time, they may lose some sense of identity in that choice. Others may find themselves drawn to various fields. One student commented on her introductory courses to two fields: "On Mondays, Wednesdays, and Fridays, I'm an occupational therapist. On Tuesdays and Thursdays, I'm a social worker." Others fail to find any one field with a compelling appeal. A Harvard student commented on the choice of a major, "Horrendous, horrifying! . . . Most of us change at least six times."[10]

Yet another student found the choice of major an exciting discovery. He notes:

I would encourage those who intend to attend college not to be too sure initially about what course of study they wish to pursue. I found many courses in college to be extremely interesting where I had found them unchallenging or even boring in high school. A good general studies curriculum for the first two years would allow the majority of students to make a more enlightened decision on their eventual major.[11]

There is wisdom in this student's observation. The changes in majors, the feelings of confusion are okay. That's what the first two years of a liberal arts education are all about—exploration. We trust that parents continue to urge their children to follow their own interests, including those areas that few of their own gender have chosen.

The choice of major may be the beginning of a lifelong engagement in a field. It may be an interest that will be soon left behind. Or it may be the foundation on which yet other choices will be made.

The Parent's Role: In all these important events in the college student's life, the parent may feel more and more left out. One may wonder, "Is there anything—beyond financing the discovering—that I can do?"

We parents live with a dilemma at this point. We who may have most to offer in aiding our young adults to sort things out have reason to feel least wanted. I (Dick) recall an experience of this type. One of my daughters was having a difficult time selecting a major in college. She was approaching the time she would have to make a choice. Since I had offered life/career planning workshops to many students, I felt I had help I could offer. So I prepared a notebook of exercises from those workshops. When she came home at Christmas, I suggested, "Honey, don't you think it would be helpful if during this vacation, you and I spent some time doing these vocational tests and exercises?" In a voice heavy with sarcasm, she answered, "I suppose so, if *you* want to." I dropped the subject, and it did not come up again during that vacation.

A year later, I was offering that life/career planning workshop in a weekend format on a college campus. That same daughter traveled three hundred miles each way to participate in it and paid an admission fee to take it! She also brought a friend along and confided to me, "Dad, she needs it even worse than I do!"

There are a number of things that parents can do. First, they can respect the autonomy and independence of which we earlier spoke. As our children are making an adjustment at this point in life, so are we. We need to learn to change our thinking about them. Our relationship changes from parent-child to adult-adult. In the parent-child relationship, one person knows what is best for the other and sees that the other experiences what is best. In the adult-adult relationship, each sees the other as competent to manage his or her affairs and as having interesting things to share with the other.

That's a delicate adjustment in a relationship but an important one. We want neither a dependent relationship nor a continually rebellious one. It is important to open the door to more mutual dialogue about these matters.

One mother shared the same advice with each of her three daughters at the beginning of their college years:

> I will never relinquish my right to give advice, but at this point you are no longer obliged to take it. I have done what I can to give you the equipment to make your own decisions. Never let anyone else tell you what to do. Never make a decision and say, "she made me do it." If you choose drugs, sleeping around, whatever, it will be your choice. Don't close any doors behind you. Don't do something because it's expedient.[12]

Of course, a parent's relationship to a child in college is not all one (parent-child) or the other (adult-adult). One student told us, "Most of the time I love being on my own. However, when I get sick, I want my mom!" Both the parent and the college student may pop in and out of these two styles of relating.

There may be a few times when a parent may need to step in and take over for a bit. A severe illness, an overwhelming depression, overly harsh heckling or hazing by fellow students (which is extremely rare), a person's being drawn into illegal activities—these might be occasions where parents need to act and extricate the college-age child. In the vast majority of situations, however, it is far wiser to encourage the young person to make his or her own decisions and then to live with the consequences.

The second thing a parent can do is to be interested in what your late adolescent is experiencing and to actively express that interest. This will take at least two forms. First, be a strong, supportive base from which your son or daughter can push off. Be in touch by letter and phone. Make clear that you, the parents, are adjusting to your child's absence. Let him or her know that you are okay. Tell about what is happening with family members, pets, home improvements. Be a welcoming sanctuary when your son or daughter pops in for a short visit or a weekend of sleeping and doing the laundry. (Don't be too surprised if the student can't wait to get home to see you, and then ignores you for much of the visit.)

There is another aspect of being a strong base for the student who is being launched. Parents need to know how distressing to the student are marital discord, divorce, or family breakup. Students worry about their parents and their welfare. Of course, adults must make decisions about marital relationships for many reasons. However, mustering as much stability as a family can provides an important base. Also, the student who is aware of struggles between the parents deserves honesty (though not necessarily a lot of details) about what is going on in the marriage.

Single parents have a responsibility as well. They may need to communicate that they are managing okay without the day-to-day presence of their college-age child.

Second, be vitally interested in your son or daughter's world of experiences. If possible, visit the campus. Take interest in the discoveries within classes and their possible connection to future decisions.

Again, avoid the parental questions, "How are your grades? Are you getting your work done on time?" Rather, ask mature, open-ended questions, "What's your most exciting course? What new discoveries have you made? What ideas are you exploring?"

We have a lot of admiration for one father. This man had never been able to go to college. He asked his daughter to send him a bibliography, course outline, and the textbooks for each course she took. In this way, he could read them and learn along with her. Some other parents invited their college students to bring home any books they found particularly interesting, after they had finished them. The parents always read enough to comment on these shared books.

Much of the learning occurs outside the classroom. Be interested in other aspects also: dorm life, roommates, activities, friends, etc.

The third thing parents can do is to serve as resources and memory banks for students. If the students seem to have bogged down or lost direction in college, parents might mention gifts and interests the students showed earlier in life and inquire whether they have investigated those interests at the college level.

Fourth, parents need to keep in mind the perspective of older young adults as they look back to these particular years in their own lives. They will recall that they did not want to feel bereft of parental interest—even during their greatest struggles to be independent.

Career Discovery on Campus: As students continue through college, they will likely develop a greater sense of their own competence, whether in the classroom or out. They will better come to know themselves, their beliefs, their commitments. While this is always an ongoing process, at this stage the young person will claim and own an identity. Such clarity will be most helpful in all decisions, including occupational decisions.

Most anticipate that such self-discovery will be translated into career plans and preparation during college. Of course, this will not automatically happen. Luther Otto and associates undertook a study of thousands of young adults for fifteen years after their graduation from high school. One thirty-year-old looks back on his college experience as something of a failure for him: "I was led to believe that if I went to college, the American dream would be mine and my life would be set. Most importantly, I thought I'd know what to do with my life. Well, here I am [age thirty] and I still don't know—and perhaps never will."[13]

Valuable as a college experience may be, it is no substitute for conscious career decision and direction. Some persons said they went to college without any clear understanding of how education related to work and that they later regretted it. A homemaker commented, "I was not career-oriented or thinking about what I would like to spend my life doing when I entered college. I wish I had a better understanding of what my education was doing for me." An electronics repair person commented,

"If I had known the possible practical applications of the subjects taught in school, I would have been much more interested in those subjects."[14]

Some were critical of the lack of preparation for the post-college world, even when they had found a fitting field. A business major relates, "Although I feel I was a success in school and was able to 'play the game' in an academic environment, I was totally unprepared to be a successful employee. . . . The rules of the 'game' in the working world were very different and were often unrelated to education and background." A computer systems analyst recalls, "The expectations I had upon graduation were smashed by the realities of a job market for which I was totally unprepared." A flight attendant explains, "I certainly wasn't taught survival skills, such as apprenticeship for a trade, or anything preparing me, specifically, for any occupation."[15]

What are we to make of these criticisms by people who felt dissatisfied with the career-preparation aspect of their college experiences? They were asking that their college experience provide them at least three things: (1) an ever more accurate understanding of what fields, subjects, topics were appropriate for them, both because of interest and discovered ability; (2) a knowledge of some possible career applications of these discoveries; and (3) some anticipation of what career experiences in those fields might be like. At very least, they wanted know how to find an entry-level job in the appropriate field.

However, not all college experiences will provide such career preparation. Seemingly, most colleges do better on item (1) than on the other two. Therefore, the purposeful student and student's family may need to discover how to improvise to fill in the gaps.

Are there things the parent can do to help? There may be. Perhaps you know persons who are working in careers related to your child's interests. If your college-age child expresses interest, you might be able to help arrange conversations, on-site visits, volunteer work, or employment during vacation periods. You may be able to discuss job survival skills. All of this might feed your late-adolescent child's hunger for appropriate vocational discovery.

While we have talked a good bit about the college experience, we'd hope for similar discovery for other young adults and dialogue with and support from parents. Parents of persons in military service may want to visit the base, meet comrades and commanding officers, and attend special ceremonies or opportunities. We know of a father who was able to meet his navy son's ship a few days out and share the last few days of a voyage with him.

Similar support and interest can be given to young-adult children who have entered the labor force. We think of one father who did this very well. After high school, his son and a group of friends tried desperately to make it as a rock band. When this young man married and had a child, he decided to work at something with more regular hours and pay, but the adjustment was hard. Over a series of lunches, the father listened and supported his son in this transition. From time to time, the father would offer a modest suggestion—for example that clothing and hair styles that fit one occupation don't fit the other, at least not for one who wants to be respected, promoted, and secure. That father applied many of the sensitive skills to supporting his employed son that others offer to their college-student children.

EARLY ADULTHOOD—FROM TWENTY-THREE TO THIRTY

Conflicting Issues

Daniel Levinson noted that in these years young adults receive two very basic but opposite messages. On the one hand, they are told to explore all the possibilities of adult living—reach out, experiment, discover, enjoy. However at the same time they are told to settle down, create a stable life structure, become responsible, make something of themselves. So contradictory are these tasks that many young adults may come to the conclusion that they have built a somewhat flawed life structure during these years. Quite frequently, around age thirty, a person stops, reconsiders, and redirects the choices made to that point![16]

Developmental Tasks

While living with these two contradictory and competing drives—to experiment and to settle—the twenty-three- to thirty-year-old has at least four developmental tasks. One of these tasks may be marriage or a committed relationship. Not all will marry, and of those who do, not all will marry in this time frame. The decision that a person is ready to marry has a number of components: having achieved some education, knowing one's earning ability, readiness to attempt a long-term commitment, and having found a potential mate.

Once married or partnered, many adjustments must be achieved. These include generating and distributing adequate finances to support the new couple, and working out a multitude of lifestyle issues—sleep patterns, food choices, sexual adjustments, spending/saving patterns, and more.

A second developmental task for married or partnered young adults is deciding whether or not to have children. Some will elect childlessness. Birth control technology has advanced to the point where couples can still have an active sexual relationship and remain childless. The majority of those who marry will choose to have children. (It is now estimated that one-fourth of all women of childbearing age will not have children.)

The arrival of a child often brings new energy into the family. The child's expressions of satisfaction, pleasure, its smiles and fledgling signs of love all add to the couple's cohesiveness.

Parenting may also add to the couple's tension. First-time parents are generally unpracticed in parenting skills. They may feel anxiety about providing for the child's safety and welfare. Further, the lack of sleep as well as the new division of and great increase in responsibilities may add to the tensions a couple faces. It is also possible that a couple will experience feelings of jealousy, competition, and abandonment with each other. The exclusiveness of the couple relationship changes with the arrival of the child.

A third developmental task is that of developing a lifestyle—as an individual if single, and as a pair if married or coupled. For the couple, the questions that must be answered and negotiated include: What are the activity levels of each partner and how do these come together? How should we balance work and nonworking hours? What activities are necessary in the nonworking hours? How shall we use our leisure hours? With what church and other organizations do we want to associate? How much energy will we invest in these? Of the roles available to each of us as adults, which shall we emphasize? And how do we work out the tensions between the various competing roles?

Employment—Career

The fourth developmental task has to do with employment. Wherever one finds oneself in the career discovery/development process, one needs to complete that journey of which we spoke earlier: specification of a vocational preference, implementation of a vocational preference, and stabilization (at least for a while) in a vocation.

The young adult will locate employment that comes close to his or her interests. There will be on-the-job training and initiation while an employer evaluates whether or not to keep the new employee. At the same time, the young man or woman also questions, "Do I want to pursue this particular occupation in this particular place?"—a decision that requires evaluating the fit between oneself and four components of the work situation. These components are:

1. *Technical skills:* Are the skills needed within my range of competence? Can I learn these skills? Does performing them give me pleasure and satisfaction?
2. *Authority relations:* Who will evaluate my work and on what criteria? What freedom do I have to set my own work schedule, and what are the limits of my autonomy? How do decisions get made around here? In what ways can I influence those decisions when they are important to me? How do I deal with the various persons with all their personality variations? How do I relate to the persons in positions of greater authority and lesser authority?
3. *Unique demands:* What are the expectations for self-presentation? for productivity? for availability? How does this all feel to me, and does this seem like a setting where I both can and want to fit?
4. *Interpersonal relationships:* What is the quality of social relationships in the work setting? In regard to my coworkers, what are the levels of cooperation and competition? How do my coworkers handle and view these factors?[17]

The answers to these questions in the workplace might be quite different from what the young person thought they would be while still in school. This may be because entry-level jobs sometimes lack satisfactions that will come in time. Or perhaps the young adult will discover that he or she is in the wrong place occupationally. If so, it is good to be aware of Luther Otto's reassuring words:

> We live in a forgiving society. People can change jobs. They need not be stuck. They can always go back to school or get new training. True, the options foreclose as we get older, but we oldsters need to remember that our young people still have time and they still have options. They have an advantage. They can always start over. Let them—indeed, help them—play out their options.[18]

Central Issue

The central issue of this stage of life is *intimacy versus isolation.* The young adult has the opportunity/need to establish an intimate relationship with someone from outside his or her family of origin. Intimacy is the ability to experience an open, supportive, tender relationship with another. One can care for another without losing one's own identity in the process. Each can support independent judgments by the other. A person develops the ability for mutual relationship and negotiation of needs with another. Each will give pleasure as well as receive pleasure.[19]

For those who marry or enter into a committed partnership, the primary person with whom to form an intimate relationship is the partner. One aspires to achieve a satisfying relationship that will be more permanent than any other. However, such relationships are not the only ones in which intimacy will occur. A growing capacity for mutual caregiving in maturing friendships will be another aspect of this basic issue in a person's life. The central process for achieving this is mutuality among peers.

Erik Erikson sees the developing a capacity for intimacy as basic to the central issue of the next stage of life. For middle adults, the issue is *generativity versus stagnation.* That is, unless the middle adult finds the capability to be concerned about, to mentor, to guide persons of future generations, he or she will fall into stagnation. Erikson summarizes:

In youth you find out what you *care to do* and who you *care to be*—even in changing roles. In young adulthood you learn whom you *care to be with*—at work and in private life, not only exchanging intimacies, but sharing intimacy. In adulthood, however, you learn to know what and whom you can *take care of.*[20]

Throughout these four chapters on vocational growth from infancy through young adult years, we have mainly been following Barbara and Philip Newman's thought. They, in turn, have brought together many people's discoveries. One key element they have used is Erik Erikson's concept of eight life stages, each with its unique life issue.

While there is much wisdom in Erikson's thought, there is also room for major criticism. As the summary quote just cited shows, Erikson says that in youth, we work on *identity,* in young adult years, we work on *intimacy,* and in middle years, we work on *generativity*—that is, guiding and influencing others. One criticism of this point of view is that it doesn't fit females. Relationships with individuals the same gender and the opposite gender is often an early and continuing concern for females. If the female bears and nurtures a child, this constitutes generativity that occurs much earlier in life than Erikson places it. Another criticism is that this construct doesn't offer a healthy style for males, either—certainly not those who seek a tender mutual relationship with a partner or child.

Christian vocation is about identity, relationships, influencing and leading others, in all stages of life. As Erikson noted, there is growth we need to do so that we may be ready to be fully functioning persons.

In the midst of all this, it is hoped the young adult can locate a fitting vocational path. This will be an opportunity to enjoy the tasks and see growth opportunities and challenges to occupy the individual for years ahead. It is likely that changes will occur at times. Persons sometimes change from careers that for some time felt like a "good fit." There may be midlife adjustments. And some people enter a post-retirement career quite different from what they did before retirement. However, those changes fall outside the scope of our attention.

For the present, the parent will be able to celebrate the successes and be supportive in the disappointments and failures of their adult sons and daughters. The parents can enjoy the friendship of their young adult children as they grow—one hopes—in acceptance and respect.

QUESTIONS AND ANSWERS

Question: What part do parents play in their young adult children's career discovery and development?

Answer: Whatever the early adults ask. Some individuals may want a great deal more input, information, discussion than others. Do not give advice unless asked for, and then in small amounts. Young adults may have difficulty finding opportunities for employment in a field that interests them. Then they might appreciate your help in helping them gain access to persons you know in the field. They will not want you to get a job for them. Still there are ways to provide access to people who would otherwise not be available to them. Your relationship with your children continues as long as you live. The ways of being supportive, encouraging, and helpful will change.

Question: When my young adult children talk about further schooling and want my help, should I provide it?

Answer: Your question causes me (Dick) to recall a vivid experience. I remember a long-suffering parent whose son had gone through several false starts, entering and dropping a few colleges and a few majors. After college, the young man could not find a job for a long time. Then, one Sunday his father came to church with a big smile on his face. "I'm so excited," he exclaimed, "Last week Johnnie got a check!"

How much schooling is enough? How much is too much? There are a few who become "professional students" out of hesitancy to leave a comfortable, well-known world and venture out. Such persons probably need to be given a nudge out into the "real world."

However, for the most part, the more schooling, the better. Our children's world will belong to the prepared, the capable, the expert. We believe that, if possible, parents will be well advised to contribute to their young adults' further education. That is, providing it is reasonable and helpful for personal and career growth. However, for those of us who are of rather modest means, decisions about further education will probably have to be our young adult children's major responsibility. We parents will provide minor but helpful aid. We believe this is a good investment. It may be wise to contribute this help early in their career even if it diminishes what we will one day give them in our will.

Question: As the parent of a young adult, now twenty-two, I have a feeling that this generation is quite different from the baby boomers, ten to fifteen years older. Am I right? Does this have implications for their career choice? for my parental role?

Answer: Many observers agree with you. A recent article characterized the "twentysomething" generation (folks from eighteen to twenty-nine) in this way:

> They have trouble making decisions. They would rather hike in the Himalayas than climb a corporate ladder. They have few heroes, no anthems, no style to call their own. They crave entertainment, but their attention span is as short as one zap of a TV dial. They hate yuppies, hippies, and druggies. They postpone marriage because they dread divorce. They sneer at Range Rovers, Rolexes, and red suspenders. What they hold dear are family life, local activism, national parks, penny loafers and mountain bikes. They possess only a hazy sense of their own identity but a monumental preoccupation with all the problems the preceding generations will leave them to fix.21

The article mentioned some discoveries about these folks' career expectations: most of all they want job gratification. They also want reasonable work expectations, from which they do not want to burn out. There is also a desire for evaluation and feedback. There seems to be an increased interest in teaching and public service as career possibilities.22

While moods do change from generation to generation, it is dangerous to generalize such populations. These paragraphs describe possible trends. However, each person should be given the dignity of being allowed to express his or her own attitudes on the matters we have mentioned.

As parents we are wise to keep an open dialogue with our twentysomething children, letting the wisdom of each generation inform the other.

Question: In this chapter, you have contended that parents of young adults still have a contribution to make in career discovery and decision. Does this also apply to their sense of faith and vocation?

Answer: We believe that parents have gifts to offer in faith/vocation as well. As with other areas, the way such help is offered will differ from earlier eras.

In the struggle for autonomy, a young adult may choose to avoid all religious groups or become an enthusiast of one quite different from his or her parents'. Trust, respect, and polite inquiry and dialogue are fitting responses to such a step.

The search for one's identity is filled with faith and vocational implications. Parents can love, affirm, encourage, listen, console when a young adult child takes blows in this search. A healthy self-concept as a child of God with gifts to offer is so basic.

We mentioned research which showed that when many persons follow the job market or something else and thus do not "listen to their hearts" during college years, they often need to make a career course correction much later. Parents can encourage/invite their young adult children to "listen to their hearts." This is being written during a time when employment opportunities—particularly for young adults—are less abundant than one might wish. Young adults may feel, particularly in such a time, that survival is the name of the game. They may not allow themselves the "luxury" of asking "What does my inner voice tell me? To what is God calling me?" Parents may be able to encourage such questioning and lend support in following the discoveries their sons and daughters make.

At least these opportunities exist to make a contribution to young adult offspring in the area of faith and vocation.

Question: You spoke of young adults' often having their children in this era. That means that we parents become grandparents! Do grandparents have anything to contribute to their grandchildren's vocational growth and development?

Answer: Yes. Young parents are often hard-pressed to earn a living, build a couple relationship, and provide basic physical needs for the child. On the other hand, grandparents may have the time to help the child experience self-discovery, be confident and trustful, and widely explore his or her own world. By this point in life, we are wise enough to do this in a helpful and noninterfering way. We grandparents know that there are few joys to match that of welcoming a new generation. Then we have a role—maybe a very small role—in calling that generation forth and seeing it unfold before our very eyes.

8

Further Ways a Family Can Enrich a Child's Vocational Discovery

Bruce Larson tells about a family where, each Christmas, the mother would give the family a new jigsaw puzzle. However, she would remove the puzzle from its original box. Family members did not know what picture they would see upon completing the puzzle. They would keep the puzzle out on a table, working on it a bit at a time.

One year, when they opened the puzzle, they were surprised that it came in a box with a picture. Surely the puzzle would be easier to assemble with that visual preview. However, as they began to work on it, confusion reigned. Gradually, it dawned upon them that Mother had played a joke on them. This year's gift had a new element of surprise—the picture on the box was not the picture on the puzzle![1]

This is a parable of what families do when helping their children discover their calling. Choices about life direction are not single decisions, nor are they just a few. Hundreds, perhaps thousands, of small decisions contribute to a career destination. One works with countless pieces of the "puzzle" (person), seeking to put together a beautiful picture with one's life.

Parents can help a child to discover what pieces he or she has and can also help the child not to forget or lose any important pieces. Parents can point out when the pieces don't seem to fit together properly and when they do. Parents don't know what the picture will look like. And at times the final outcome is quite different from what they had anticipated.

However, there comes a point where the analogy breaks down. In a person, the pieces of the puzzle can fit together in several different ways, all of them appropriate. The pieces can expand or shrink. The combinations can change. What seems the best way to draw things together at one time may not be best at a later period. As interesting as a picture puzzle may be, an even greater fascination is the mystery of a person's life and vocation!

We now seek what further enrichment parents can give their children in performing an important task. That is, drawing all the components of their unique selves together into a life plan.

We interviewed a number of career counselors about how they applied their knowledge and skills to their own families. We will now present their responses, adding insights from other sources.

How can you enrich your child's vocational discovery and development?

A Parent/Counselor's Overview

In *Choosing Your Career, Finding Your Vocation,* author Roy Lewis, a pastoral career counselor, pauses to note the role of the family in this discovery. He reminds us that the family is the most powerful social unit that forms who we are as adults. "The roots of our career direction and occupational choices are clearly found throughout the early development of the individual and the impact that the family has on us."[2] He points to the story of the birth and early life of Jacob (Gen. 25 and following) as a clear example of this.

Lewis suggests that there are four lessons/discoveries of vocational importance that the family communicates to its children. The first is awareness of each child's self-worth. It is hoped that each family helps each child feel good about himself or herself. Second is the area of communication skills. In families, persons learn to speak, to listen, and to work out differences. Third is the understanding of the importance of rules. In every family, there are spoken and unspoken family rules. One needs to learn to recognize rules, to address them, and to make one's peace with them. Fourth, the family teaches how to relate to people and institutions outside it. In a family we begin to formulate our world view. We learn either to withdraw from the world or to "see society and the world around us as open, hopeful, a place to dream, to work, and to contribute."[3] We will come back to some of Lewis's points and elaborate upon them in this chapter.

SEE THE WHOLE PICTURE

Suppose your child asked for your encouragement in pursuing four activities, and somehow you knew that one activity would be an important part of a future occupation, one would be part of some cherished leisure moments, one would lead to formation of some central values and commitments, and one would be forgotten and never pursued again. You knew this about the activities, but you did not know which activities would fall in which categories. Would all four be worth pursuing?

It is important that parents keep the whole picture in mind, both for themselves and for their children. An occupation is an important part of a person's picture, but it is not the whole picture!

Viktor Frankl has suggested that the most primary search of every person's life is the search for meaning. He suggests that there are at least three kinds of values in which one can find meaning in life:

1. *Creative values:* what a person *gives* to the world as regards one's work and creations.
2. *Experiential values:* what a person *takes* from the world as regards encounters and experiences.
3. *Attitudinal values:* the *stand* a person takes as regards the issues and tragedies of one's life.[4]

Frankl underscores the need to be concerned with the whole valuing person. Richard Bolles speaks of three areas of life—work, leisure, and education—which need to be balanced throughout a person's life.[5] As a parent, you can keep in view the total person as you participate in your child's growth and development. You can encourage attention to all aspects of your child's self.

Someday when your child chooses a first occupation, there will be at least some disappointment. The disappointment comes from the occupation's incapacity to express all that the person is. At that point, you as parent may be able to say, "Your occupation is an expression of who you are. But it by no means expresses all of you. Your family membership, your leisure, your volunteerism, your citizen involvement, your faith, your dreams and visions—all this and more makes you who you are."

One parent/career counselor we interviewed recalled the quote, "There are two gifts we can give our children. One is roots. The other is wings."

HELP YOUR CHILD OWN HIS OR HER SPECIALNESS

There is an experience that saddens me (Dick) every time I observe it. As a clergyman, I have occasion to spend time with a group of teenagers. I enjoy being with them—they are talented, attractive, and witty. But as we begin talking, I discover that these winsome folks often have low opinions of themselves. This experience reminds me that we caring adults can do more to help the children and youths we love experience their specialness.

By contrast, I recall a wonderful line from Mr. Rogers on his television show. He would look out at the children watching him and say, "You make it a very special day, just by being you!" That is called a "being stroke." Would that every child, youth, and adult received a few being strokes every day! "I'm glad you exist. Do you know you are good company? I like being with you. Let's . . . It will be more fun if we do it together."

Parents can offer this gift to their children. Parents who greatly love their children will find countless ways to communicate this. As a matter of fact, Dean L. Hummel and Carl McDaniels catalog thirteen parent behaviors that promote a feeling of worthiness in their children:

    a. Respect: for their ideas, interests, attempts at self-expression.

    b. Responsiveness: to content and feeling expressed in a child's ideas. (This includes being aware of one's own bias and not projecting it on the child).

    c. Empathy: perceiving and understanding and being a part of the child's world and the child's dreams.

    d. Acceptance: of who they are (being strokes) and what they attempt to do (doing strokes).

    e. Trust: demonstrated through acceptance of self-expression, self-assessment, and fantasies.

    f. Expressiveness: clear, understandable communication that conveys trust and acceptance and allows for differences.

g. Dependability: being there and providing the necessary support, encouragement, ideas, or ways of validating the child.
h. Consistency: so the child knows reliably what to expect.
i. Perceptiveness: acting in a way that confirms that the parent understands the child's interests, ambitions, and goals.
j. Genuineness: honesty, including confrontation when necessary, but without negativeness or put-downs.
k. Positiveness.
l. Objectivity: helping and allowing the child to see oneself objectively, to face reality, to weigh pros and cons.
m. Sensitivity: acting in a way that the parent's behavior will not be perceived as a threat.[6]

Barbara Sher, in her book *Wishcraft,* comes at this issue from an equally useful perspective. In a chapter titled "The Environment That Creates Winners" she invites the reader to reflect upon the family in which he or she grew up.

She asks, "(1) Were you treated as though you had a unique kind of genius that was loved and respected?" She comments that the answer "yes" to this question is all too rare.

Then she continues: "(2) Were you told that you could do and be anything you wanted—and that you'd be loved and admired no matter what it was?" This, she says, is love in action—to respect a person, to allow that person his or her own fantasies and expressions with encouragement. She notes that too often parents enter into premature evaluating of these dreams.

She continues, "(3) Were you given real help and encouragement in finding what you wanted to do—and how to do it?" Sher points out that this one is tremendously important, because even if a person is given number 1, and number 2, they may not have been much use without the help implied in number 3. The helps given a young child may be very basic—books, library cards, and guidance where books of interest may be found, toys, tools, craft material, etc. The important thing is the message: There is a way to get where you want to go. I, your parent, am willing to explore that way with you.

Then she goes on: "(4) Were you encouraged to explore *all* your own talents and interests, even if they changed from day to day?" If you wanted to be an actor one day and a firefighter the next, did your parents encourage you to investigate and explore and help you do it? The key word is "explore."

Then: "(5) Were you allowed to complain when the going got rough, and given sympathy instead of being told to quit?" Were you allowed to complain—with persons who would listen, support, and let you make your own decision what to do?

"(6) Were you bailed out when you got in over your head—without reproach?" Many get help from their parents when they ask for it. However, most parents have to throw in a little "reproach"—advice or scolding. As Sher notes, "Trying something and messing it up is a complete and self-contained learning experience." No parental comment is needed.

And finally, she asks, "(7) Were you surrounded by winners who were pleased when you won?" She points out that the atmosphere that calls forth winners is almost always made up of winners. Winners are not necessarily famous people or stars. They are people who are "contented and curious, open and vital, . . . trust life and respect themselves." Such persons allow and encourage others to try their own unique experiences.[7]

Sensitive parents may want to ask Sher's seven questions to explore the family atmosphere they have built. They can then see if their home environment creates and recognizes winning children.

One parent we interviewed commented, "Basically, we support, enjoy, and have a great deal of pride in our children."

Each of these authors nudges parents to affirm and call forth the specialness of each child.

DISCOVER WHAT YOUR CHILD ENJOYS

Vocational psychologist John Holland once noted that even with all the sophisticated vocational tests, there is one highly reliable way to know whether a person will be content and successful at an occupation. That is simply to ask, "Do you enjoy it?"

Enjoyment is central and basic to career choice. Usually, using the skills that we do best is enjoyable to us. Since we have more skills than we can use in any one occupation, some may be more enjoyable than others. Joy in doing things, fun, ecstasy—these are experiences of which to be aware.

What activities attract your child like a magnet? Where does your child find joy? At what does your child have fun? What does he or she really like doing? Is there any pattern to this? Is the joy in the activity itself, in the company of folks with whom the activity is done, or in the struggle and achievement? You can't teach your child what brings joy—your child can teach you. Don't try to separate "leisure" joy from "work" joy. Many people have eventually discovered how to make a living by doing what they once enjoyed only as a leisure activity.

How fortunate are those persons whose work involves many activities they truly love doing. I (Dick) am one of those fortunate people. I enjoy drama, music, reading, thinking, public speaking, teaching, talking with folks, helping people work out problems, getting close to people, and exploring beliefs and values. I do all those things and am paid to do it! (Of course, there are aspects of my work that I don't enjoy, but the percentage of tasks I do like is high.)

As parent, you can be sensitive to the activities and experiences that your child deeply enjoys. You can help your child be aware of this as well. Together you may be able to use it as "radar" to help your child discover ways to act on this occupationally.

Play with Your Child throughout Your Lifetimes

Bill Page, an educational consultant, has summarized much knowledge about play in the following statement, entitled "The Difference That Play Makes." He notes that "Play builds a sense of personal power." In self-directed satisfying play, a child discovers he or she can plan, make decisions, control, and create.

Further, "Play enables children to build social relationships." In the area of play and "let's pretend," the child has a safe place to try on roles, express feelings about family conflicts, death, loss, and to face fears and anxieties.

Also, "Play builds a base of experience which is the foundation of competence." Fantasy play can allow the child to experience a rich variety of situations, people, objects, sounds, sights for association and expression.

And again, "Play teaches children to value differences." In play, children see the natural and wonderful diversity of what others think, do, make, and are.

Further still, "Play, like nothing else, builds confidence in use of the body." In play, children throw themselves into an all-absorbing use of their bodies, experiencing speed, agility, balance, self-expression, and the sheer pleasure of physical well-being.

Moreover, "Play enables a child to find his or her own powers of concentration." In play, a child finds a focus that is based within the self. A sad contrast is the child who is heavily dependent for structure on adults and/or watching TV.

He continues, "Play develops the spirit of curiosity." In play, a child wants to find out about things just for the satisfaction of it, not in response to others' demands.

And finally, "Play is the heart of rejuvenation." It is the source of discovering freshness in the world, of personal renewal, of experiencing quality of life.[8]

Play is important for children of all ages, for youths, and for adults. A valuable gift exchange can occur in the realm of playfulness. Parents can share with children their own styles and types of play. Children can, in turn, teach the same things to their parents. All of these styles can be used in discovering each family member's calling. The important thing is to invite your child into your play and be open when the child invites you.

Ann Kaufman asks:

> Are you a playful person? Are these things happening in your life right now? Laughter . . . surprises . . . special secrets . . spontaneity . . . time for 'unplanned' time . . . serendipity . . . time alone . . . a friendship with a child . . . a friendship with a playful adult or adults . . . special private rituals for pleasure for yourself (i.e., bubble bath/shower, good food, a walk alone or with someone special . . .) a change in routine . . . time with an older person . . . exposure to something new.[9]

She is pointing out to us that there are possibilities in play beyond what we may have discovered. Discovering more play possibilities for oneself and one's child is enriching indeed. For example, some folks are able to make routine tasks into play.

A special opportunity for parents is to share with children any sense of play one experiences at work. Are there times of triumph? a good bridge foursome or ping-pong game over the lunch hour? some fun people you work with? practical jokes? ridiculous things that happen on the job? Children will love to be let in on the joke. This might have a small part in forming their attitude toward work.

Cindy, a psychiatric nurse in a private facility, recalls an experience of this type.

> Recently, I stopped by work on my day off to pick up my paycheck. My senior high daughter, Jennifer, was with me because we were going to shop together. At the psychiatric facility, they were celebrating with a Hawaiian Day—both patients and staff. When I walked in, my Director of Nurses sprayed me with a water pistol. As we went to the office, many staff had grass skirts over their clothing. Both patients and staff had imitation leis and bright colors on. I acquired a water pistol too and surprised my coworkers (who were in the office doing reports) squirting them. It was fun, and I thought it neat for Jen to see.

I (Dick) recall a time when a close friend was scheduled to come and give special leadership to my congregation. My daughter, a middle-high student at the time, persisted in begging to be allowed to go with me to meet him at the airport. "Why do you want to go?" I asked, "Because you guys are nuts!" she responded. She had seen where work and play came together for me and wanted to be in on it. It bears repeating—play, joy, enjoyment are major signposts on the road to one's vocation.

HELP YOUR CHILD DISCOVER AN EVER-EXPANDING WORLD

Occasionally a friend invites me (Dick) to view some photographic slides or home videos. Perhaps these pictures are of a trip, an event, or of their family. As a fellow photographer, I enjoy this experience, but invariably I walk away asking myself two questions: "Why did they aim their camera where they did? Why did they pick these particular scenes to show me?" Some principle of choosing—perhaps conscious, perhaps unconscious—went into those decisions. Out of unlimited possibilities, they have picked a few selections and shown me their world.

As a parent, you have a similar but grander opportunity. You will show your children your world. When your children are small, you will choose what of the world they will experience. And in so doing, you will teach the attitudes that will influence what they will see and discover when they become independent. Your children will make vocational choices informed by what they know of the world. You are the one who will open that world and influence what aspects of it they experience, at least to some extent. That is a magnificent but awesome responsibility!

Each of the career counselor parents had discovered ways to share important parts of the world with their children. Here are few of the things they said:

"Very early, we communicated our love of books and libraries. We took our children to the libraries often, got them cards, and helped them find books that were pleasurable to them."

"We took our children to where we work. We wanted them to see the place where we worked, the activities we did, and the people with whom we work."

"We wanted our children to know persons of all nations. And so we invited exchange students, international visitors, and missionaries to our home."

Another parent mentioned that one of her children was accepted as an exchange student in Australia. She commented: "We felt sharing Beth with the world was worth our losing her to our home for a year."

Another parent mentioned how stimulating it had been for her college-aged daughter to spend a year traveling with "Up with People." The chance to work with an international cast and to travel widely both in the United States and overseas was broadening. The opportunity to be in many service institutions and to observe various types of service occupations contributed to her personal poise and confidence. It also helped clarify her college major and career goals.

"We love to travel and plan family-oriented vacations that include some 'learning is fun' activities (zoos, museums, nature trails, etc.)."

Several parents mentioned encouraging their children to participate in YMCA groups, scouting, and 4-H. One parent credited 4-H with contributing a great deal to her children's leadership skills.

Another parent spoke of his children's participation in the program called "Outward Bound." One experience that his son particularly remembered was a three-day period in which he was alone, without food and only water. He had these three days to do as he willed. The parent felt that this program stirred in his children a confidence and resourcefulness that few other experiences had done.

"We wanted our children to know persons of other ethnic groups and economic classes. And we wanted them to know persons who were victims of injustice in our land. And so we invited such persons to our home and visited as a family in theirs. We took our children to see things that people were doing to improve their conditions. As a family we visited things like food cooperatives and Habitat for Humanity projects. We found ways that we as a family could be involved—such as a march to protest unfair rental practices."

One parent commented on the new worlds that are near at hand— perhaps in our own homes—that we miss. He suggested, "If a car tire is flat, who is most apt to fix it? Probably the person with the most experience. However, that knowledge might someday be very useful to the family member that doesn't know how. Why not take the time to teach that family member to do it?"

Two parents came out very differently on the subject of discovery through employment during adolescent years. One parent commented, "We did not encourage any working on jobs (except baby-sitting) during the school year. This was due to the need to spend evenings in homework preparation." (Another parent concurred, noting that disciplined rehearsal and practice—whether in sports or in the arts—was much like work. Further, the student might generate scholarship support by doing that well). But another parent commented, "Our boys always had to work and to get their own jobs. We felt this was of value, even if it was a negative, 'I sure wouldn't want to do that for the rest of my life.'"

"Our children enjoyed music and drama, and so we tried to expose them to the best. First we took them to children's concerts and children's theater. Then later to full symphony concerts, ballet, and theater. Though one considered a music career, these arts are now an avocation for each of them. We feel their lives were enriched both by what they saw and heard and by their school participation in such activities."

The above list shows what a few parents have done to open the wider world to their children. Some of those activities might be something that another parent would want to try. Others might stimulate one's own ideas. Every parent can resolve to begin opening up the child's world.

Then the parent can teach some attitudes and skills so that the child will continue the investigation.

ENCOURAGE YOUR CHILD'S DISCOVERY OF HIS OR HER INNER WORLD

In addition to the world "out there," sensitive parents encourage their children to discover the world "in here," the world of creativity and skillfulness. Recognition of such gifts and their development are crucially important for a person's vocational becoming. Parents make such affirmations as these:

"If my toddler bursts upon me with a Santa Claus suit that she has improvised and created out of clothes in her closet, I will pause, praise her, and take her picture."

"If my child wants to tell me a joke, I will laugh or smile. If invited to read a story he has written, I will listen, read, and encourage."

"When my child fantasizes about the wide range of things she will be, places she will go, achievements she will accomplish, I will fantasize along with her. There's plenty of time for reality testing."

"If my son is fond of snakes and wants to have a snake in a cage in his room, I will cooperate. This may make me uneasy, particularly feeding it live mice, but his delight in his snake makes it worth it."

"If a child shows any inclination to singing, musical instruments, or dancing, I will encourage. I will do this by helping the child find opportunities to explore that interest. I will encourage the person's fullest possible creative development. I may have to endure through renting, buying, and selling several different instruments. Let the discovery expand! I will take an interest in daily/weekly progress, attend recitals and concerts, and share the joy of music and dance."

"If my child is fascinated with mechanical things, I will tolerate and make space for the half-assembled objects. If the interest is in art, I will help make space for that kind of clutter."

"If my child loves to participate in sports, I will be in the cheering section as often as possible. My task will be to affirm and celebrate, not to evaluate the performance or criticize the sportsmanship. I will leave that to coaches."

David Campbell, in *Take the Road to Creativity and Get Off Your*

Dead End, speaks of families that stimulate creativity in their children. He concludes with several suggestions.

First, Campbell says, "Surround your children with stimulation in the form of *ideas.*" Tell what you think about important topics in life, but be clear that these are your ideas, not necessarily TRUTH. Let them know others have other viewpoints.

Give your children stimulating gifts. More important than money for these gifts are imagination and energy. Gifts might include books or helping the child to write his or her own. Other gifts might be hand tools; plants; pets; musical instruments; scientific gadgets; sewing machines; and tickets to operas, plays, performances, concerts, and lectures. Another stimulating gift can be one's time, teaching a child how to use the tools or instruments at hand.

Make sure your children meet innovative adults. Introduce them to folks you admire at work and other places.

Travel can stimulate creativity. An Arabic proverb says, "If you love your children, send them on their travels."

Develop their fantasy. Stimulate their imagination. Make up stories together. Enjoy the creations of others.

Then, Campbell says, relax! It will probably be more an inviting atmosphere rather than deliberate efforts that will contribute to the child's creativity.[10]

MODEL, TEACH, AND EXPECT RESPONSIBLE LIVING

There are at least two areas in which you as a parent may want to encourage responsible living. One is the broad area of reliability, punctuality, promise keeping, etc. These qualities are known as "self-management skills." People are often hired because they demonstrate these qualities and skills. People are frequently fired for the lack of them.

Therefore, attempt to be that kind of reliable person with others and with your children. When you work with your children on family tasks, attempt to embody these characteristics and help them do so. And in the promises you make to your children, live out these qualities faithfully. Hold your children accountable for these qualities as well. Then it may be that your child will come to assume that this is the way to live.

The second area is that of education and learning. Commit to life-long learning. Your curiosity, the way you keep growing personally and in skills are important examples. Communicate and demonstrate these traits to your children.

Be equally committed to your child's education. Be eager to hear about your child's school experiences. Inconvenience yourself to participate in parents' orientation sessions and teacher-parent conferences. When elective courses are chosen, discuss the choices and know the reasons for your child's decisions. If your child is either very advanced or having difficulty with some subjects, be involved. Explore—with your child—what educational opportunities are available to respond to your child's circumstance.

MODEL AND TEACH DECISION MAKING AND PROBLEM SOLVING

So far, the discussion has focused on expanding one's concept of world and self. Another task is to direct this information into ever-smaller channels. Having generated a great deal of information, then one must decide what to do with it. After all, a person can be in only one place at a time, pursuing one course of study, performing one job.

And so one must ask, "Of all the dreams I have had, which dream do I want to pursue first? Of all the possibilities that hold some appeal for me, which do I choose for primary investigation?"

For a person with many gifts and possibilities, this may be the more difficult part. It involves saying no to some tantalizing possibilities. I (Dick) remember the agony of one of my daughters, who was a senior in high school at the time. After having researched colleges and applied to her four top choices, and having been accepted at all four, there came decision day. She liked what she saw of all the schools. How could she decide to say no to three of them, and yes to just one of them? It was a tearful, tension-filled day until that decision was made. The happy conclusion is that she felt good about her decision. She stayed at that school, received an excellent education, and met many fine people who continue to this day to be her friends.

A poster proclaims the slogan, "Not to decide is to decide." While there is some truth to that statement, more likely, conscious, intentional choice will lead to the more enjoyable calling. And so as a parent, you will do well to help your child learn how to make decisions.

Gordon Porter Miller, an authority on decision making, points out that there are some poor ways of decision making. One is doing the first thing that comes to mind. Another is to make the decision with a "me-first" mentality—that is, looking only for what is fun at the moment. And still another is to look only to the immediate consequences. (His example is the teenager who may elect to take only nonacademic general courses in order to have more free time in high school. This student may not have considered the impact this choice could have on college admission or future goals.)

Miller suggests there is a basic seven-step process for much wiser decision making. He insists that this process can be applied to most decisions, that it can be modeled within a family, and that it can be taught to each age of child from preschool through adolescence. The steps he suggests are:

1. Establish your *values.*
2. Set your *goals.*
3. Identify possible action *alternatives.*
4. Collect *information* on all possibilities.
5. Look ahead to *consequences* and how they can be managed.
6. Take responsible *action,* the best alternative for you.
7. *Review* the action taken.[11]

Hummel and McDaniels suggest a family process for aiding one's child in career decisions. Their process includes five steps, using the acronym "SWING." They suggest:

*S*tudy self: Help your child develop a sense of worth and esteem. Help the child to know his or her personal values.

*W*in awareness: A person must have awareness of who he or she is and what he or she can do.

*I*dentify information: Accurate information—firsthand information if possible—about oneself and about one's possible careers and/or schools is essential.

*N*egotiate plans: Using all the above factors, develop plans and take charge.

*G*ain experiences: All of the above may be influenced by both external and internal change. And so the time will come when one needs to go through the process again.[12]

You, as parent, need to be available to your child not only in the decisions made, but in helping the child learn how to make good decisions. How do you do this? For one thing, by allowing children to make as many decisions as are fitting at each stage of their lives. Then, let them live by the consequences of their decisions. Unless they are in big trouble, don't bail them out when they don't like the consequences of their decisions.

One father mentioned that he felt it important to ask his children the "impertinent questions," such as "If your values are —————— then why are you —————?" He felt that was important not only for exploring a particular action but in learning how to think critically about important behavioral questions.

There is another skill that persons need as well—that of problem solving. Suppose one makes the right decisions but somewhere along the line encounters barriers to further progress. What then? Richard Bolles has suggested, "Always have a 'Plan B.' "[13] But, before giving up Plan A, there may be some problem-solving skills to apply. And perhaps parents can help with that.

One career counselor/parent told us:

> I think there was one time I used my career guidance skills with my own child. That was in helping her solve a problem that seemed impossible. She wanted summer employment in a field related to her major field of interest but had not been successful. And she was about to give up. I suggested to her a couple of techniques I teach, "networking" and "field surveys." That is, I urged her to go talk to some of my friends and acquaintances. She was not to ask them for a job. Rather she was to tell of her interest and ask both for suggestions and for other persons with whom to visit. She did this quite faithfully for a couple of weeks. In the process she found the kind of summer job she wanted. She treasured that experience, not only for the work but for the discovery that sometimes problems can be solved and doors opened.

As a parent, you too, want to be available to your children, ready to resource with all the problem-solving skills you have.

CREATE AND/OR OFFER AND/OR ENTER INTO
CAREER DISCOVERY OPPORTUNITIES

One career counselor father felt quite strongly that parents should attempt to obtain courses on career decision for their children. Through his expertise, he was successful in getting one offered in the school his children attended. He felt that this was important to his children. If the school does not offer such an opportunity, the local YMCA, community college, or some churches might offer a course. At least a few parents have taken the course along with their children. In such an experience, they have discovered grounds for many fruitful discussions as well as some informed decision making.

One mother found a resource for this planning that excited her. It is entitled *Choices: A Teen Woman's Journal for Self-Awareness and Personal Planning.*[14] Through her women's business and professional group, she was able to have a course offered to young women, using this resource. This is a twelve-session experience using a journal/workbook to explore a wide range of topics, including: attitudes and awareness; financial needs and planning; values and goal setting; decision making and assertiveness; marriage, children, and family planning; skills; nontraditional careers; and career and education planning.

Another woman who taught middle-high Sunday school obtained permission to use *Choices* as Sunday school curriculum. Still another woman worked with her women's group to gather mothers and daughters into an exploration using this same resource. In each setting, participants tell of growth in self-awareness, intentionality, and mutual support.

There is a partner volume for males, entitled *Challenges: A Young Man's Journal for Self-Awareness and Personal Planning.*[15] It has exactly the same outline and chapters as *Choices,* but is geared to more specific male concerns.

One father did not feel he had the expertise to create or lead a career course. Still, he found a "door of opportunity" to engage his son in significant discussion on these topics. He knew how much his son enjoyed computers, computer programs, and computer games. He was delighted to learn that his community's school system offered career discovery programs on computer. These programs were available both in the guidance counselor's office and as one option to explore in the computer application class required for graduation at his son's high school. His son readily agreed to work through this program and to do printouts of any pages that seemed interesting or helpful. These pages formed the basis for the best discussions he and his son had on these all-important subjects.

The particular program his son took was *Discover*.[16] In this program, there are interest, abilities, experience, and values inventories. These are combined to help the student discover possible occupations and fitting schools where one may gain preparation. Some students simply use the program to locate colleges that meet their most basic interests and needs. Another program is *Guidance Information System*.[17]

We applaud these efforts but would add one modest caution. Parents can become so excited about career discovery that they force classes or vocational testing on children before they are ready. It is wise to know about such opportunities and to offer them to teenagers and young adults. However, young people must decide for themselves if this is something that feels valuable and if they are ready for it.

MODEL, TEACH, AND INVITE FAITH-FULL VOCATIONAL LIVING

There was a set of qualities we saw in the career/vocational counselors we interviewed that they did not speak of. Perhaps they were too modest, or perhaps it was so much a part of them that they didn't even notice.

What we refer to is that these were persons of faith. They received strength from and gave strength to churches of their choice. They sought God's guidance on their own careers. They were ready to respond to the cries of others, whether clients, community, or family. They had ways of strengthening their inner life through prayer and meditation. Further, these persons recognized that the demands of their vocation often drained them. When that happened, they had specific, conscious ways of seeking rest and renewal from their faith resources.

Whether lay persons or clergy, they lived their lives as vocation, as calling from God. Children born to their families were thus invited into compassionate caring for others and being in touch with the source of their faith and tenderness. Following them, each of us will want to claim our faith resources for the difficult and important task of parenting. Especially, we will want such strength to convey a vocation vision for our children.

BE HEALING, PATIENT, FORGIVING OF YOURSELF AND YOUR CHILD; LIVE WITH FAITH, HOPE, AND LOVE

One counselor/parent with whom we visited spoke of her three children. She recalled their struggles as adolescents and their eventual career decisions (which were still in process). She celebrated the rapport she now enjoys with them. Knowing the project on which we were working, she advised us to tell our fellow parents, "Things happen in spite of us. There are so many other influences, multiple options, and unexpected outside occurrences for us to expect to have that much influence. Tell the parents not to do a lot of 'Social Engineering.'"

That woman spoke with a wisdom born of experience. We want to hear what she has to say. If we have implied that this will be smooth, safe, and easy for either the parent or the child, we have misinformed you.

Your children also may "blow" some decisions. Even when they make appropriate ones, they may not follow through as adequately as we parents might like. Other issues may often take center stage, demanding much of the child's attention. The road to identity, intimacy, and productivity will probably be a bumpy one with several detours. Your child may choose to follow one of those detours rather than the well-traveled road you as a parent had anticipated. And possibly, your child may choose some vocational destination in spite of you—not because of you.

You, as a parent, will possibly mess up a few opportunities, also. You may want to affirm and support your child and wind up smothering instead. You might attempt to give freedom and autonomy and to call forth self-direction in your child, but possibly you will overprotect, second-guess, and snipe at what your child chooses to do. You may intend to be supportive and understanding when your child makes mistakes or disagrees with you. Instead, you may wildly overreact. You may do too much or too little, or say too much or too little.

All of this may call for healthy doses of forgiveness. You may need to forgive yourself as parent and offer reconciliation to your child as well. This may require you and your child to have faith in each other and in the quality of the love between you, even when it is not entirely visible. Also it will require a faith in a God who reconciles, forgives, and gives each person new beginnings and fresh starts.

There may even need to be forgiveness for some harmless things. For example, a child may discover that she or he is quite different from parents as regards skills, interests, or values. That child may feel the need to be "forgiven" for being different. One father suggests that with such children, the parent needs to clearly communicate, "You're certainly not a chip off the old block; you're so good at————— . That's good. You don't have to be like me to be okay."

One of the things that will keep both parents and children from being at their best in all this is fear. For the child, it may be fear of the future, fear of competing, fear of failure: "I know what the present is like, but what will the future be like if I step out on this risk?" Many a parent, too, fears letting go. A parent may also draw back fearfully from the parenting style described here, knowing how far he or she now is from that style. Take heart—all of the rest of us are far away also. However, we have a deep love for our children and a trustful vision of their possible futures. So give it your best shot as much of the time as you can manage.

As a parent and a child work together on the puzzle of that child's life, maybe they don't know what the picture will look like. Perhaps it is different from what either expected. That's okay—more than okay. As you have loved the child, you will love the evolving picture of your child/adult/friend in vocation.

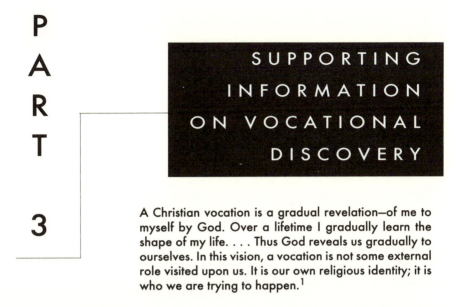

PART 3

SUPPORTING INFORMATION ON VOCATIONAL DISCOVERY

A Christian vocation is a gradual revelation—of me to myself by God. Over a lifetime I gradually learn the shape of my life. . . . Thus God reveals us gradually to ourselves. In this vision, a vocation is not some external role visited upon us. It is our own religious identity; it is who we are trying to happen.[1]

How does God speak to me and reveal me to me? Scripture affirms that God speaks to us through history—the history of our world and our individual personal histories. Reflection on these inner and outer histories and projections of what might happen in the years ahead are helpful in discerning one's vocation. The world of work has become more complex and stressful. To find one's fitting occupation and vocation at any moment is an intricate and delicate task.

Fortunately, there is some help at hand. Vocational psychologists have at least some preliminary wisdom. They can help us understand the process of discovery. They also have discovered some ways to gain a reasonably good fit between ourselves and our workplaces. Furthermore, a variety of disciplines have come together to help anticipate the major directions in employment opportunities in the future. This section contains a brief summary of such wisdom.

Possible Road Map for Reading Part 3. We authors have had this knowledge as a background for all that we have written to this point. You may want to browse through these pages (subheadings will help you find what interests you). Or yours may be a more intense interest than we can satisfy here. The works cited will guide you in beginning an in-depth study of these matters.

9

What the Experts Can Tell Us—Process

A Christian vocation is a gradual revelation—of me to myself by God." In this chapter we will invite students of vocational discovery to describe how this revelation takes place. We will weave together the contributions of significant persons in this field:

1. Donald Super is a pioneer in guidance and counseling. His teaching and published writings span more than four decades. His research has included observing persons' careers develop over time. He has also offered an overview on vocational choice.
2. Richard Bolles is a clergyman who investigated the best possible information to help out-of-work friends find new employment. He has put many helpful discoveries and theories into a cohesive and practical plan for discovering career direction. From his writings and his workshops, thousands of people have been helped to find creative new directions. Many career counselors have been trained by him. Bolles is vividly aware of the Christian perspectives on calling and vocation. He sees these processes as part of the way in which a person discovers one's calling.
3. There are a number of people who enrich and complete this picture.

WHAT IS AN OCCUPATIONAL CHOICE?

Donald Super says that a person's choice of occupation is a statement of understanding who he or she is. A satisfying choice of occupation should involve two basic tasks: (a) gaining as clear and accurate an understanding of oneself as possible; (b) gaining a thorough knowledge of the occupations that would give one self-expression.[1]

WHEN DOES THIS DISCOVERY OCCUR?

How does a person's self-concept develop and become translated into occupational goals? Super notes a number of processes involved, beginning in infancy and continuing throughout one's lifetime.

1. *Exploration* is the first phase for an infant and continues throughout life. The infant explores and discovers both its body and its world, while the adolescent discovers possible new skills or activities.
2. *Self-differentiation* also occurs in the small child but continues in adolescence. A person discovers his or her own uniqueness and difference from other people.
3. *Identification* involves trying to be like another person, either unconsciously or quite consciously and intentionally.
4. *Role playing* follows identification. The small child identifies with a parent and tries to imitate this parent. Or the child may identify with and imitate others. This may be in imagination or in behavior. Either way, the child is trying new roles to see how valid the roles are.
5. *Reality testing* emerges naturally out of role playing. Child's play, school courses, extracurricular activities, and employment all offer reality-testing experiences. These in turn strengthen or modify self-concepts.
6. *Translation of self-concepts into occupational terms.* Eventually, a decision is made on the occupation that reflects the person's true self.
7. *Implementation* into a specific plan of education and occupation is the final step.[2]

Parents may have more specific questions: When should these various steps occur? If one of these stages has not happened by a given time with my child, are we in trouble? Do we then need some sort of corrective actions?

Vocational psychologists respond with broad understandings of when these stages occur. They note that persons vary widely in these steps, within a quite normal range.

For example, Super divides entire life histories into four stages: growth stage, from birth to about age fourteen; exploratory stage, covering approximately from ages fifteen to twenty-five; maintenance stage, from ages twenty-five to about sixty-five; and decline, beginning at age sixty-five. That doesn't help very much!

With more precision, Dean L. Hummel and Carl McDaniels have described the childhood and youth developmental phases in choosing a career as follows:

Fantasy Phase, before Age Eleven

During this period of development, children believes that they can do whatever they like. Their own needs and desires, their fantasy and play are what determine the possible occupational choices of which they speak. Parents can listen to their children's expressions of such dreams and enter into the fantasy games in which they act out jobs. Mimicry may both be a way of exploring and an early expression of creativity.

Tentative Phase, Ages Eleven to Seventeen

During this period of development, other considerations enter into the thinking and planning of children/youth. Since not all of these considerations have been reality-tested (and indeed some of them cannot be), choices are tentative. Parents will be wise to accept their child as a growing person, regardless of strengths and weaknesses. The parent might help children explore various fields and jobs that are expressive of what they are saying about themselves. This should be done regardless of the parent's previous experience in such occupations or the parent's opinion of those occupations. Children will need the experience of discovering for themselves. Hummel and McDaniels suggest that this period may have three substages.

> **Interests (about ages eleven to twelve):** During this time, interests may well be the first basis for choice. However, there is the growing understanding that ability is necessary as well. Parents will want to offer all the possible resources they can muster to help children explore their interests.

Capabilities (about ages thirteen to fourteen): Increasingly, children begin to be consider their capabilities along with their interests in making plans. Of course, knowledge of their capacities is not total, and choices are tentative.

Values (about ages fifteen to sixteen): Values may begin to be more a more powerful influence in the choice process at this stage.

Transition (about ages seventeen to eighteen): At this point, these factors are brought together and integrated as adolescents continue to explore choices. The choices continue to be tentative. However, there is the awareness that they must make choices that have some impact on their future.[3]

While Hummel and McDaniels's description seems too precise to us, they have located the general flow of occupational development for children and youths.

WHAT ARE THE BASIC ELEMENTS IN THIS CHOICE?

Donald Super has identified six factors that enter into one's vocational choice.

Aptitudes

The first factor is the field of aptitudes, the capacities or potentials of the individual. These aptitudes tend to be stable during the youth and adult years, when vocational choices are being made. Aptitudes affect career choice and success in a number of ways. People seem drawn toward occupations that use their best aptitudes, and they may be happier there.

A surprising discovery is that sometimes great aptitude (or intelligence) for a field is not as much of an advantage as one might imagine. Beyond the specific needs of a given occupation, the greater aptitude helps one learn faster and make quicker adjustments. However, beyond that, additional intelligence or aptitude doesn't seem to be much of an advantage. Success in that field will depend on other factors.

There is a most important discovery here. Some students may not catch on right away and may have to struggle to master a subject. These students may wonder if they can succeed in a given field. However, they may have as great chance of success as those who catch on right away and get A's without effort!

Interests

The second factor is the field of interests. There is a strong tendency to enter and remain in fields that provide adequate outlet for one's interests. And so to know oneself well as regards interests is most important.

Aptitudes and Interests Combined

Richard Bolles has gathered some useful information about how aptitudes (for which he uses the term "skills") and interests come together. Following the lead of Sidney Fine, he points out there are three families of skills:

(a) There are *Self-Management Skills*. These refer to how one manages life, gets along with others, relates to space, time, impulses, etc. To speak of one's self-management skills is to describe one's humor, tact, sensitivity, etc. For example, picture a person who can get to work on time. This person can take orders and criticism, work without supervision or under close supervision, and dress appropriately for the task at hand. Such a person also gets along well with coworkers. This person has demonstrated several important self-management skills. More people are hired because of self-management skills or fired for the lack of them than any other reason. Bolles sometimes calls this type of skill "environmental skills," pointing out that it is wise to find the work environment that matches one's self-management skills. This is something that a parent can help a child discover. Does the person like to work in groups or alone? in structured or unstructured situations? closely supervised or unsupervised? indoors or outside? The recognition (and development) of self-management skills and matching them to a fitting work place is an important component in career self discovery.

(b) There are *Functional Skills*. These are the skills one has as regards information (or data), people, and things. These are what most people call "aptitudes." These skills exist across time. They appear in childhood and remain with a person throughout one's lifetime (sometimes dormant or rusty, but still there). For example, suppose a child had problem solving skills, revealed in being able to postpone bedtime. That child, now an adult, still has problem solving skills. Such skills are transferable from one field to another. These are some of the skills that make us most adaptable, able to do a wide variety of jobs. Quite often persons are unaware of their greatest functional skills. They use them so unconsciously and automatically, they are not even aware they have them!

(c) There are *Work Content Skills*. These are the skills using memory, the things one has been taught (by others or self). One may gain such skills in school or elsewhere. These skills refer to one's knowledge of the content of a course one has taken. Such skills are related to performing a job in a particular occupation, field, or profession. Knowledge of a foreign language, the parts of an engine, or a particular accounting procedure are examples of work content skills.[4]

Bolles points out that each person has a wide variety of skills. In fact, each person has from five hundred to seven hundred skills. The marketable combinations of these skills are nearly endless. It becomes important to know, own, and claim these skills in oneself. Workshops offered by trained counselors across the country teach students to recognize these skills by identifying satisfying accomplishments in their own lives. Then, with the input of others, the students are helped to locate the skills used in that achievement. Sensitive parents may be able to do this with their children. Adults can help a child recognize and claim skills as events unfold in the child's life.

Aptitudes plus Skills Used with Enjoyment

Since a person has so many skills, it makes sense to use skills that one enjoys using. A key question is "What are the skills you have and enjoy using?" Bolles points out that enjoyment isn't a fluke—rather it is part of God's plan. Our Creator wants us to eat and designs us so that eating is enjoyable. Our God wants us to love and possibly to procreate and so designs us that we enjoy sex and delight in love even more. God gives us unique skills and abilities. When we use these skills, we enjoy doing so. Enjoyment of skills is what Bolles calls "Divine radar" for locating fitting career decisions.[5]

Skills recognized, claimed, and enjoyed form a most important component in a fulfilling career choice. They are also a vital part of God's guidance in this choice.

We have given close attention to aptitudes-skills and to interests-enjoyment, since they are most significant factors in choice. There are others that we can list more briefly.

Personality

The third factor in career selection is personality. We will defer our discussion of personality to the next chapter.

Family

The fourth factor is the family. It contributes to shaping needs and values and provides both positive and negative role models. In the family, patterns of work, play, and interpersonal relations are established. The family rallies its personal and financial resources to help the child become.[6]

Since the family generally has been an ignored factor in career decision, this whole book attempts to expand on the family's contribution.

Economic Factors

Fifth, there are economic factors. These include such matters as supply and demand, business cycles, tastes and styles, national priorities, fads, and "acts of God." These also involve depletion of natural resources, public policy and priorities, unionization, organization of business enterprise, and socioeconomic status.

Chance or Accident

The sixth factor is chance or accident. This refers to circumstances external to the individual that have some influence in vocational decision. Perhaps up to one-fourth of people in the work force come to their employment by chance or accident. This may be okay for some—there are folks who don't have all that strong a preference and can make do with any work that provides a living. Others may discover their choice of employment either was a "happy accident" or wasn't as much chance as they thought. These persons wound up in a career that was quite fitting to them. However, for the most part, a person will be better pleased if a career is purposefully chosen.

HOW DOES THIS COME TOGETHER?

How does all of this come together for the individual? Super suggests that a "synthesis" takes place—a synthesis of the personal needs and resources of the individual with the economic and social demands and resources of the culture.

We can summarize much of what we have said by turning to two concrete images. Both come from Richard Bolles. One is the cart, the horse, and the road. This image suggests the three questions each person will have to ask. The cart stands for what you have to offer—the skills, knowledges, values, and commitments you bring to any task you do. The horse stands for where you wish to use what you have to offer. The road stands for how you identify the place you would like to work, the way you get hired there.[7]

The other image is that of a flower—one with a center and seven petals. This flower represents you as a person. You need to make the discoveries about yourself that you can describe in the center and petals of this flower.

We urge you to look at the flower diagram in Bolles's *What Color Is Your Parachute?* (page 210 in the 1995 edition) or in one of his "quick job-hunting (and career-changing)" maps.[8] For now, we will describe the flower for you. You may want to sketch it for yourself.

Two of the petals explore the setting in which you would like to work. Petal A looks at geographical locations that may energize you as well as specific work conditions. Petal B invites consideration of the spiritual or emotional setting you want as a work environment.

Petal C considers rewards. What range of salary, leadership, responsibility do you desire? What other rewards are important you?

Three petals explore the tools or means important to the person. Petal D examines what people-environment is important to you. Think about the people you will serve as well as the people with whom you will work. Petal E has to do with your favorite kinds of information, both in regard to content (what do you have knowledge about that you take delight in?) and the form (or medium) of the knowledge. Petal F gives you the opportunity to record "Kinds of things I like to use these skills with."

Petal G gives consideration to outcomes—both immediate and long range (the latter having to do with goals for life).

The center of the flower is given to one's most basic skills—with things, with people, with data or information.

These are the basic questions in the discovery of any job or career. They are the ones your child will need to answer in a simple, basic way in gaining his or her very first job. They are also the same questions you will need to answer in a much more complex way in considering a career change.

WHAT'S WRONG WITH THE INFORMATION IN THIS AND THE NEXT CHAPTER?

We have tried to collect good and comprehensive information in this overview for parents. However, we are aware of a flaw in what we have presented. Most of the available information was written by males from a male point of view, based on observation of males.

This is true of the developmental psychology we have cited. Carol Gilligan has noted, "Implicitly adopting the male life as the norm [the psychological theorists] have tried to fashion women out of a masculine cloth. . . . In the life cycle . . . the woman has been the deviant."[9]

It is also true that much of the vocational psychology that has informed us has a male-studying-males bias. Regrettably, the counterpart information does not seem to yet exist. In their groundbreaking *The Career Psychology of Women,* Nancy E. Betz and Louise F. Fitzgerald survey a large literature on different aspects of women's career issues. However, they are forced to conclude, "There is as yet no satisfactory theory of the career development of women."[10]

They point out that the theories we have cited have some relevance to women's career development. Preliminary work has been done. However, they add, "additional, and in particular, more comprehensive theories are needed. Further advances in our knowledge of women's career development will require theoretical innovation and synthesis."[11]

Their work locates a number of variables where women's experience is different from men's. They point out that until quite recently, a large proportion of women did not expect to work after their children were born (and most expected to have children). There is thus the lack of encouragement of serious career exploration. Further, there may be few role models in many careers and much sex stereotyping as to what careers are fitting. Lower compensation, job ceilings, and sexual harassment and intimidation are still other barriers. All of this points to the fact that for a woman to develop a strong vocational identity and persist in it is more subtle and complex than one might realize.

I (Helen) have worked in a number of positions during my career. I am happy to see some real progress in career development opportunities for women.

There has always been a disparity in the compensation of men and women, but the ratio of women's wages to men's has improved from approximately $0.55/$1.00 to $0.70/$1.00 in the years I have been working.

Women have traditionally been limited to participation in the lower-paying jobs. This is gradually changing. I know several women doctors, lawyers, retailers, politicians, ministers, broadcasters, and astronauts. It is encouraging to see women in such places of leadership, even though the difference in pay remains considerable. Young women will still need a healthy dose of self-confidence to gain the necessary education and buck the "old boy" system.

An aspect of female vocational discovery that needs creative attention is the plight of the poverty-stricken single woman with children. Dropping out of school, teenage pregnancy, and drug use may possibly have contributed to these women's situation. Whatever the cause, there is a great need of strategies for these women's career discovery.

There are some things happening to make things better for women. Passage of Title 9 in the 1972 Education Amendment prohibited discrimination in educational institutions. While it has not been as uniformly applied as one might wish, at least that ruling is there.

Women's organizations have taken several helpful steps. The National Federation of Business and Professional Women established a council on the future of women in the workplace. Its charge was to recommend methods of improving opportunities for working women and preparing women for their future lifework. The American Association of University Women commissioned a study of girls in schools, which has been used to work for change in public educational policy. The National Organization of Women has participated with major corporations to bring about a "Take Your Daughter to Work Day." It is held in April each year. This is but part of the ferment that is changing women's work environment and possible career development.

In her essay "Women's Barriers and Opportunities," Norma Carr-Ruffino lists the hindrances of which we spoke and then goes on to list advantages and opportunities of being a woman in the workplace. Her list includes:

1. Communication skills in both oral and written expression, particularly of expressing feelings.
2. People skills—the ability to be good listeners and experience

empathy with others, nurturing, encouraging and supporting others.

3. An affiliation need, which leads women into establishing work environments where workers participate and feel empowered.

4. Intuitive skills, which are extremely valuable in understanding people and predicting what they might do next.

5. Less ego involvement, less total identification with one's job success, and thus, possibly more ability to resolve conflict, lead teams, empower others.

6. Visibility—being the first, only, or one of a few women in a male-dominated field may provide special opportunities for gifts and contributions to be noticed.[12]

With this, we have said as much as we know about the additional subtleties and complications of vocational discovery for women. We are sure that there is much more to be discovered and said.

This concludes the first part of the psychological discovery we promised you. We will continue this discussion in the next chapter. There, we will consider two alternate ways to understand your child's personality and the connection between personality and career choice.

QUESTIONS AND ANSWERS

Question: My child has "chosen" an occupation, and she's only ten! She seems enthusiastic, talks about it often, and reads whatever she can find about it. I feel this is too young to know. What do you think? What would you do if you were I?

Answer: I would relax. Your child will have plenty of opportunity to test this choice against reality over the next years. Parents will want to avoid two traps. They should not be so enthusiastic about a child's occupational preference that the child feels "locked in," unable to consider other alternatives. Nor should they be critical of the choice. If they are, the child may feel pushed into an "I'll show them; I'll do it in spite of them" position.

I should tell you that I (Dick) made an occupational choice at age ten that, for the most part, stuck! After the death of my prime role model, my father, I stated that I wanted to do what my dad had done. That is, I wanted to be a minister. This was either a remarkably good guess or an appropriate choice. I later came to feel that this awareness was the beginning of my vocation, my call. Areas of emphasis have changed over the years, but I am in the occupation I chose at age ten.

I also know a person who is enjoying a challenging career in pharmacy. This person "knew" he wanted to be a pharmacist at age six. At six, he loved to go spend his allowance each week at the corner drugstore. He never talked of any other career and is prospering in his choice.

Question: My problem is just the opposite. My son is twenty-one and has finished his sophomore year of college. However, he doesn't seem to know what he wants to declare for a major, much less choose as a career! What should he and I do?

Answer: Your son has several choices. He can tentatively elect a major, with the awareness that he may need to change his mind. He can withdraw from school for a time and seek some employment that might help him explore some possibilities. He can volunteer for a term of military service. He can devote a block of time to some voluntary service that might lend experience to a possible area of interest. Often parents are appalled when their children want to interrupt their education for a year or more. However, this may be a wise choice, so that they can make fitting the decisions about education. College handbooks now term this "stopping out." Approximately one-fourth of all college students interrupt their education for a semester, a year, or more, taking more than four years to achieve an undergraduate degree.

Choices of major and possible career may be less ominous for your son if he realizes that his choices need not be for a lifetime. Indeed, many persons make a number of career changes. His question is simply, "Where do I want to start?" It will help, also, for him to recognize your patience with him and your partnership with him in these decisions.

Question: I'm still not sure what you are saying to me in this chapter. What should I do with this information as I raise my child?

Answer: This chapter may serve you and your child in a number of ways. First, it may sensitize you to some basic processes of living that have implications for career choice. Next, it may give you some patience with the process and help you know that you don't have to hurry it. Finally, it may encourage you to observe your child's interests, skills, and developing abilities. You may want to think about what these mean for career possibilities. Observe what your child really loves to do, what gives the child joy and enjoyment; then think about career possibilities around those activities. It will be good to discuss those possibilities with your child from time to time.

10

What the Psychologists Can Tell Us— Personality

"Christian vocation is . . . our own religious identity; it is who we are trying to happen." Vocational psychologists have helpful tools to help us know who we are. They ask such questions as: How can the personality be known? In particular, how can we understand the interaction between personality and vocational choice? Are there things we can know that can aid our children—and us—in making decisions that will be wise and fitting?

Two pioneers have asked such questions and have formed helpful personality theories.

JOHN HOLLAND

John Holland was a vocational rehabilitation counselor for the veteran's administration. After working with thousands of clients, he noticed groups of persons with similar characteristics, interests, and needs. Out of this, he proposed a theory which he and others have researched and revised. The result is a widely used and respected concept of vocational choice.

Holland's Theory

From his research, Holland has discovered the following factors.

Personality Types: In our culture there are six basic personality types. These are realistic, investigative, artistic, social, enterprising, and conventional. These personality types are briefly described as follows:

- Realistic types are practical, thrifty, and prefer concrete rather than abstract problems. They may prefer being outdoors and working with objects, machines, tools, plants, or animals.

- Investigative types are analytical, precise, intellectual. They think through rather than act out problems and enjoy observing, learning, investigating, evaluating, and problem solving.

- Artistic types are expressive, original, sensitive, intuitive, and innovative. They prefer self-expression through artistic media, using their imagination and creativity in unstructured settings.

- Social types are friendly, helpful, and empathic. They like to work with people with the hope of informing, enlightening, helping, training, or curing them. Often they are skilled with words.

- Enterprising types are ambitious, extroverted, and self-confident. They, too, like to work with people but with the goals of leading, managing, influencing, or persuading.

- Conventional types are careful, orderly, accurate, and attentive to detail. They are willing to carry through another's instruction with their clerical, numerical, or accounting skills.[1]

Actually, no one is just one of the types. Each of us is a combination of all six types in descending order. Your personality is in some way a combination of those priority choices. In his many writings, Richard Bolles pictures a "party exercise." Imagine you come to a six-cornered hall. In each corner are a group of people who are all one of these types. Which would you pick as the group with whom you would most enjoy the party? If that group leaves, which group would be your second choice? your third choice? Your answers give you a quick intuitive hunch as to your Holland personality type.

Work Environment: There are also six kinds of work environments. They are described below:

- In the realistic work setting, explicit physical concrete tasks are required. Persons may need mechanical skill, persistence, and physical movement, often outdoors.

- In the investigative work setting, there are tasks that require abstract and creative abilities. Persons need imagination, intelligence, and sensitivity to address physical and intellectual problems.

- The artistic work setting is often unstructured. Persons are asked to interpret or create artistic forms through taste, feelings, and imagination. The worker must draw upon all of his or her knowledge, intuition and emotion.
- The social setting has problems that require the ability to interpret, help, cure, or modify human behavior. The worker needs an interest in caring for and communicating with others.
- In the enterprising work setting, there are tasks where effective use of words is needed to direct, persuade, lead, or sell.
- In the conventional work setting, there are tasks and problems that require systematic, concrete, routine processing of verbal and mathematical information. Skill and attention to detail are required.[2]

Of course, work environments are like personalities—none is of one pure type. Rather a work environment includes a combination of elements from each of the types in some descending order.

Personal Expression: People look for those work environments that allow them to express their personality. That is, persons want to use their best skills and abilities. They like to work in places compatible with their attitudes and values. People prefer work situations that give them opportunity to take on agreeable problems and roles.

A Good Fit: When one finds a work environment that matches one's personality, good things happen. One will be happier and stay longer. Furthermore, one will be more content, effective, and productive. Therefore, it is important to know one's personality type and to find work environments where that personality will fit.

How Choice Can Go Wrong or Right

Holland has also discovered where vocational choice can go wrong. It may go wrong if:

1. A person has not had enough experience to gain clearly defined interests, competencies, and self-perceptions.

2. A person has not had enough experience to learn about the major kinds of work environments.
3. A person has had unclear or conflicting experience as regards his or her interests, abilities, or personal characteristics. For example, a child can have a bad school experience in a subject where he or she has good skills and possible interest.
4. A person can have unclear or conflicting experience as regards work environments. For example, some aspects of a given job may be real turn-offs for the young worker. However, this undesirable part of the job may be totally unrelated to the environment for that kind of work.
5. A person may have a slow rate of development or a complex outlook that makes choice difficult. Again, a person may have a sense of alienation and therefore an unwillingness to choose.[3]

Holland also identifies where vocational development can go right for the child or youth. As one might suspect, it is exactly the opposite of the points where one can go wrong. Career choice will go right if there are: adequate opportunities to know oneself; enough experience to know some occupational environments that might fit one; therefore, accurate self-knowledge and knowledge of the work environments.

What This Means to a Parent

For the most part, this is a commonsense theory, aided by John Holland's gifts of observation and classification. What does a parent do with it? For the most part, a parent can simply offer a child a wide range of activities. Then the adult can note the ones that the child delights in and selects repeatedly. These might give clues for future vocational choice.

Here are some examples of activities of children in each of Holland's six personality types:

Realistic: wants to be outdoors . . . spends time with pets . . . likes gym and sports. Wants to know how things work—will take things apart . . . gardens or grows plants.

Investigative: asks "why" a lot . . . likes to figure out how ideas go together . . . interested in science . . . full of questions.

Artistic: loves inventing with art, music, dance, or drama . . . doesn't like to stop when told it's time to quit . . . loves color and movement . . . doesn't like to raise hand in class . . . sense of humor . . . flexible thinkers, minds go off in different directions.

Social: will teach pets or dolls . . . set up play school with younger children . . play nurse, play doctor . . . keep a dairy, scrap books and photo albums . . . enjoys talking or writing for the fun of it.

Enterprising: enjoys being with friends . . . likes to lead in games . . . takes charge, makes the rules . . . likes to be in programs or plays . . . likes to argue . . . tries to win . . . sets up lemonade stand.

Conventional: good at math . . . does work neatly and accurately . . . follows teacher's instructions . . . will have toys and games in neat order . . . keeps track of how much money he or she has and how it is spent . . . likes to be timekeeper for activities . . . likes to be on time.

Here are a few samples of activities in which youth might engage according to each of Holland's personality types:

Realistic: goes out for athletics . . . is enthusiastic about Scouts or 4-H . . . works on cars . . . enjoys shop courses, home making, cooking, sewing.

Investigative: competes in science fair or joins math team . . . likes open-ended assignments, depth in learning . . . may be class historian.

Artistic: enjoys acting in school play, but also happy painting sets in background . . . enjoys music and dance . . . will practice long hours . . . not leaders . . . may be thought "off the wall" . . . unique or original ideas . . . may invent school pranks.

Social: may help in preschool . . . be hospital volunteer . . . report or edit for school paper . . . keep a diary . . . baby sit or pet sit . . . tutor others . . . enjoy church activities, especially mission service trips.

Enterprising: runs for class or school office or runs campaign for a friend . . . enjoys debate . . . sells newspaper or yearbook ads . . . sells greeting cards or stationery.

Conventional: makes lists . . . keeps calendar . . . operates computer efficiently . . . wants to understand assignments and follows directions . . . likes structured activities.

A parent observes the child/youth selecting activities, increasing in skill, and enjoying these activities. Together, parent and child make important discoveries. There is some hidden wisdom here—skills used and enjoyed may give clues for possible choices of careers.

When a child reaches adolescence or young adulthood, she or he might want more precise guidance. To this end, there are vocational tests that are based upon Holland's theory. The most popular are the *Strong-Campbell Vocational Preference Test*[4] and John Holland's own, *The Self Directed Search.*[5] These are often available in the guidance or counseling offices of high schools and colleges. By taking one of these preference tests, one learns one's three-letter Holland classification type and is introduced to some possible careers that might be compatible to that personality type. It is by no means the end of a search, but it can provide useful information for beginning it. These tools can provide a few more clues in career discovery.

ISABEL BRIGGS MYERS AND KATHARINE C. BRIGGS

Katharine Briggs was a woman who, at the turn of the century, was intrigued with the similarities and differences in human personality. She had begun to develop her own typology when she discovered and read Carl Jung's work on psychological types. Mrs. Briggs quickly accepted this system and began to explore it and elaborate it. In time, her daughter, Isabel Briggs Myers, took up this work. Myers sought for a way to put this theory to practical use. She decided to develop a testing device that would be a "type indicator." The result of this labor was the *Myers-Briggs Type Indicator.*[6] In time, this paper-and-pencil inventory exercise has become one of the most widely used personality measures.

It gives information about personality styles and does not search for personal problems. Unlike John Holland's work, this is not primarily a career guidance theory. It is a personality theory with wide usefulness. It has implications for marriage or partnership, child rearing, education, leadership, improvement of communication, and more. Here we will simply sketch out the Myers-Briggs concept and suggest its relevance for career choice.

The Theory in Brief

Briggs and Myers proposed that differences of behavior are the result of differences in mental processes. They located four pairs of these mental processes and gave a name and an initial to each. Again, when we learn who we are from Myers-Briggs's perspective, we will have another set of initials—this time four letters. (Some of the letters are the same as Holland's but mean different things, so keep these two methods separate.)

First, they note two basic orientations to life, *extroversion* and *introversion*. These two terms are often misunderstood. Regretfully, these have become confused as social styles. People think of the "hail-fellow-well-met" style or the shy, withdrawn individual. However, this is not what these terms mean in this usage. They refer only to *where we focus our attention and from where we gain our energy.* Is our greatest interest in the outer world of people and things or the inner world of ideas and concepts? Which energizes us most?

Extroversion is seen in children as the need to be with people and to be busy. Extroverts must experience. They learn by doing in order to understand or appreciate both things and concepts. Adult extroverts are verbal, accessible and understandable; they are people of action and practical achievement.

Introverts are the opposite. They focus on the inner world of concepts and symbols and often find it difficult to express themselves. Action comes only after consideration and is governed by subjective values. Whereas extroverts are energized by their people contacts, introverts draw their energies from a different source. They will "charge their batteries" from working quietly alone, reading, meditating, participating in activities that involve few or no other people. Either of these (introvert or extrovert) combines with and is influenced by the other three pairs of mental processes.

Within each of these orientations, there are two possible attitudes (or styles of responding to information)—judging and perceiving. Here the key question is: "Do I prefer closure and the settling of things and getting things done, or do I prefer to keep options open and fluid?"[7] Some persons want to have plans and routines; set goals; have a matter settled, a decision made, a deadline met. In Myers-Briggs terminology, those persons have a judging attitude. Other persons show curiosity and want to stay with the process, learn more, gather more information, and are in no hurry for closure. These people would be described as having a perceiving attitude. Again the terms may be misunderstood. Judging persons are not judgmental!

For each of these attitudes there is an accompanying pair of mental processes, sensing/intuiting and thinking/feeling. Let us consider each of these pairs in turn.

The sensing/intuiting pair has to do with how one gathers information and benefits from it. Think about one of your children and ask, "How does this child learn?" Is it through the five senses? Does learning come by touching, looking, smelling, tasting, and seeing? Does the child prefer to memorize rather than reason? Do things have to have an immediate, practical purpose in order to catch his or her attention? If so, this is an individual who comes to an understanding of the outer world through sensing. Further characteristics include liking routine and knowing the "right" way to do things.

In contrast, the child you are focusing on may learn by perceiving patterns and meanings, seeing possibilities. Intuitive perception involves imagining, memory, and associations. This child likes new ideas and activities and dislikes routine. Further, such a child anticipates and jumps to conclusions. The intuitive readily grasps the meaning of symbols and thus finds reading easy.

The thinking/feeling pair answers the question, "How does a person make decisions?" When thinking is the preferred process, one prefers objectivity, logic, and action based on reason. The thinking child asks for objective explanations for everything and sees cause-and-effect relationships. She or he tries to be "fair," but in the process is impartial and impersonal. This child will be more truthful than tactful. If another's feelings are hurt, the child is often unaware of it.

When feeling is the process used in making decisions, personal, subjective values come into play. The individual is more concerned with personal relationships than things or ideas and permits feelings to overcome logic. This individual will be more tactful than truthful and may conform to the group in order to avoid disharmony. Though concerned with others, this individual needs approval and personal support. (The terms are again misleading. Many feeling persons are good thinkers and excellent students.)

We have now described each of the four pairs in the Myers-Briggs Type Indicator. Here is a visualization of the relationships among these eight possible characteristics:

Life Orientations

Extroversion   Introversion

Mental Processes

Gathering information   Making decisions
Sensing/Intuiting   Thinking/Feeling

Attitudes

Perceiving   Judging

Type theory states that one has a preference for one or the other of the processes within each of these pairs. Of course, people need to be able to use both sides of each pair. However, one part of each pair will be like the figure in the middle of a focused picture. The other part of the pair will be like a slightly out-of-focus background. Some of these processes will come easily and feel natural to a person. Others will feel like an uphill struggle.

Very young children use these attitudes and functions in a seemingly random manner. However, a preference within the sets will become clear early in the child's life, possibly by or before the age of six. As the preferred processes become apparent, they need to be allowed to develop, to be perfected. If this is allowed, one process will be dominant and provide the unifying element in the individual's life. However, since one must use each of these processes at least occasionally, the less-preferred processes should not be entirely neglected. With maturity, all of the functions need to be allowed some development.

Our intent here is to present some ideas that contribute to an understanding of individual differences. We hope for an understanding that will promote the emergence and development of your child's unique approach to life. The following is a presentation of the characteristics of each of these elements of type.

LIFE ORIENTATIONS

Extroversion	*Introversion*
Energized by interaction with people	Energized by solitary activities
Understands by experiencing	Understands by questioning, quiet contemplation
Likes new experiences	Hesitates before new experiences
Approaches new people and experiences without hesitation	Likes to be alone or with one person
Is interested in other people and their activities	Is interested in ideas and concepts
Eagerly responds to interruptions	Dislikes interruptions

Is eager, confident	Is cautious, reluctant
Gets impatient with slow jobs	Works on one thing for a long time
Takes freedom of movement for granted, thus can seem to intrude unawares	Can appear withdrawn, is not intrusive
Spontaneous, verbalizes quickly	Rehearses responses internally
Expressive, enthusiastic	Likes quiet space

MENTAL PROCESSES

Gathering Data

Sensing	*Intuiting*
Learns through use of five senses	Uses words and symbols for learning
Attends to the concrete	Explores possibilities
Likes facts	Is imaginative
Enjoys using established skills	Enjoys learning new skills
Likes routine	Is impatient with routine

Memorizes	Likes to do things differently
Likes facts	Jumps to conclusions
Focused in present	Future focused

Making Decisions

Thinking	*Feeling*
Impersonal	Personal
Logical	Permits feelings to override logic
Concerned for objective truth	Concerned for people
Wants authority, justice, structure	Likes warm, personal relationships
Deals with ideas, things	Motivated by others' needs
Is more truthful than tactful	Is more tactful than truthful
Seems not to know how one's actions affect other's feelings	Naturally friendly; wants to help others; responds to needs

ATTITUDES

Judging	*Perceiving*
Life is to be: willed, decided, settled	Life is to be: experienced, understood, flexible
Tells you what you ought to do	Asks, "What do you do?"
Has a system for doing things: wants order, structure	Is open minded, seeks to understand
Interested in essentials only	Asks, "what? why?" Is aware of the still unknown, always seeking more information
Sets "shoulds" and "oughts" for self	Is adaptable, tolerant
Has enduring friendships	Takes on new friendships easily, drops friendships easily
Wants and observes deadlines	Seldom is aware of deadlines

Can you identify your child's preferences? Think back on your child's day. Reflect on your child's chosen activities; playmates (or lack of them); ways of coping, learning, deciding. Are you beginning to surmise your child's Myers-Briggs personality type? Can you discern the differences from one child to another? There are sixteen different potential combinations in Myers-Briggs type theory. Each child is unique, even while sharing a personality type with others. Cherish!

At the same time, we all must at times use our least-preferred functions and need to be encouraged and provided opportunities to do so. For example, encourage your young extrovert occasionally to engage in an activity that can be done alone. Without overwhelming your introvert, provide opportunities for interactive play. A word of caution is in order here: because the majority of individuals in our society are extroverts, the introvert may need help in protecting his or her right to peace and privacy. She or he may need some extra assurance that being oneself is good. While the extrovert/introvert preference develops earliest, the thinking/feeling preference shows up early, also. Unfortunately, it sometimes appears in the form of family conflict. The young thinker understands logic and wants reasons for doing things. The feeling type may not respond to your logical explanations but rather do things to please. While using the approach that appeals to your child's personality type is best most of the time, vary your approach. Expose your feeling child to cause-and-effect logic and your thinking child to the value of pleasing.

The sensing child learns best by actually doing. Therefore, while using intuitive skills, such as pretending, won't be easy for such a child, it can be both useful and fun occasionally. The intuitive can be helped to appreciate the actual by emphasizing what can be learned and enjoyed through one's senses.

Advantages Parents Gain by Having This Knowledge/Sensitivity

"That's the way *I* treat a virus!"

There are at least four advantages for parents who are aware of type theory and correspondingly sensitive to their children.

First, parents become more able to accept a child as that

child is. Children may have quite different temperaments from their parents and from their brothers and sisters. Parents may be troubled or confused by such differences. One child may love to be hugged and cuddled and be equally anxious to please; another child may not want to be touched and demand a logical explanation for each parental request. That may be the difference between your feeling child and your thinking child.

Similarly, a parent may be embarrassed if the child has difficulty meeting new people. If the child shows hesitation, hides behind a parent, refuses to speak when meeting someone new, a parent may fear that something is wrong with the child. However, the child may simply be expressing in a raw way what new situations feel like to an introvert. In time, the child will need to develop some extrovert skills. However, the child should not be forced to become an extrovert.

Psychologists caution that the introverted child is particularly vulnerable to damage if asked to behave as an extrovert.[8] David Keirsey states the matter strongly and keenly. "ABANDON THE PYG-MALION PROJECT," that endless and fruitless attempt to change the other into a carbon copy of oneself. "It's OK to marry your opposite and beget children who are far from being chips off the old block, but it is not OK to take marriage and parentage as license to SCULPT spouse and child using yourself as a pattern to copy. PUT DOWN YOUR CHISEL. LET BE. APPRECIATE."[9] There is great gain when we parents learn that lesson. Then the child will be able to grow and develop in the manner that is fitting and appropriate.

The second benefit is that the child may move more easily toward self-acceptance. Reassurance by the parent that it is okay to be who the child is can be so helpful. The various types are not evenly distributed throughout the population. For example, 75 percent of the population is extrovert; 25 percent introvert. Many introverts recall having thought as a child and youth that there was something wrong with them. Likewise, intuitive children (also a 25 percent minority) sometimes confess to feeling like ugly ducklings. Parents' acceptance and affirmation of children can help them be at ease with themselves and thus to grow and develop more fully.

Third, the parent can help the child deal with educational difficulties and enhance the child's educational experience. For example, sensing children may have difficulty with school for a number of reasons. They may not comprehend the symbolic nature of letters quickly and thus fall behind in learning to read. They have far too little hands-on learning experience and become bored and withdrawn. They tend to do poorly on tests, since they may not work as quickly as others. For these and other reasons, they tend to withdraw from school earlier than some others. A parent with awareness of this can help the child achieve and cope. Possibly, when electives become available, the student can be guided into learning experiences that are more compatible.

Fourth, being aware of one's personality type has important implications for career decisions. Isabel Briggs Myers noted, "A . . . destructive conflict may exist between people and their jobs, when the job makes no use of the workers' natural combination of perception and judgment but constantly demands the opposite combination."[10] On other hand, career choice is enhanced if one finds opportunity to exercise and improve one's preferred processes.

Let us give a few examples. Persons with the sensing-thinking combination are well represented in the fields of accounting, banking, finance, and commerce. Persons with the sensing-feeling combination are found in large numbers in sales, customer relations, nursing, and education. Persons with the intuitive-feeling combination are likely to be creative writers, ministers, counselors, health professionals, and journalists. Persons with the intuitive-thinking combination are heavily concentrated in research and applied sciences and the law.[11] No one should feel limited by such observations. The appropriate question is , "What are my preferred mental processes, and where can I use them?"

QUESTIONS AND ANSWERS

Question: I still don't understand why my children are so different from each other. Can you explain that by these theories?

Answer: Not really. Not even the experts agree on how much is the disposition we are born with and how much is affected by our surroundings. However, how we became the way we are is not the important part. What is important is that each of us be accepted as she or he is. There are no "good" or "bad," "right" or "wrong" personality types. All are good. And all have fitting occupational opportunities.

Question: That makes me think of my daughter. She is a nice person who enjoys people and they enjoy her. However, she isn't interested in school work. She makes average grades or worse. Are you telling me there's hope for her?

Answer: Indeed we are! You are possibly describing an extrovert in the Myers-Briggs classification, and perhaps either an enterprising or social preference in the Holland category. People skills are valuable gifts and in high demand. Of course, there will be need for some other knowledge as well. So encourage her in her studies. But don't panic.

Question: I'm not sure I can describe my children according to either of these types. Are there tests that will help us know where they fit in these categories?

Answer: Yes, but they are neither needed nor appropriate for children in the exploration stages of life. Vocational preference tests are often available in high school years from guidance offices and in college counseling offices. Vocational psychologists can make such analysis available, if in adolescence or young adult years more careful reflection is necessary. If your child is preadolescent, simply observe and enjoy. You may be fascinated to see diffuse activity come to resemble some of the preferences we have mentioned.

Question: If I feel my child is denying who he or she is in a career choice, what do I do? Do I intervene? try to talk my child out of it?

Answer: That depends on the age of your child, the seriousness of the faulty perception, and the depth of the career choice. We wouldn't worry much about fantasies or small steps toward careers that may not fit. If this is a step with a lot of commitment in it, then it's different. Encourage this person to do reality testing. Suggest that he or she talk to persons in that line of work. Offer opportunities to observe persons in this field in their workplace.

However, rarely will parents have that drastic a task. Much more often, their task will be to help children know that it's okay to be whoever they are. Who you are—that is part of your calling, your Christian vocation. God made you that way for a purpose.

11

Significant Employment Trends: What They Mean to Your Child

Consider these recent headlines:

Families Make Ends Meet by Moonlighting at Home
Tomorrow's Global Economy
World Population Milestone: Triumph or Threat?
High Tech Job Maker, or Job Taker?
North American Free Trade Treaty Ratified

In this, the "Information Age," information can be only too available. Yet this describes the fast-changing history of our times. Scripture affirms that God calls out of history, out of the events of one's day. And so, sorting this knowledge out and making it useful is a primary task for those who would prepare for the future as a person of vocation.

The one constant is the fact of change, which in the world of work is accelerating. Many of us now have jobs that didn't exist for our parents. Our children in turn may experience the appearance and disappearance of several jobs in their lifetimes. As we assist our children in vocational discovery, we do well to anticipate what future needs may exist.

INFLUENCES AND TRENDS

What influences created and will continue to shape this fast-changing world? There are at least four outstanding areas of major influence:

1. Technology
2. Economic conditions

3. Population growth and decline
4. Changing lifestyles

Each of these contributes its share of headlines daily.

Technology may be the most important source of change. The rapid development and application of computer electronics and other technical breakthroughs have brought about changes in almost all areas of life. These factors will even more drastically affect how those things will be done in the future.

Andy Hines points out that information technology—"infotech" for short—includes many parts: computing, telecommunications, networking, expert systems, imaging, automation, robotics, sensing technologies, and mechatronics (embedding microprocessors in products, systems, and devices). These technologies are coming into practically every area of work. Infotech will reshape how workers do their jobs, providing them with new tools. It will also change the nature of jobs as organizations redesign jobs to take advantage of these capabilities. Some estimate that there will be more change in many job tasks in the next five years than there was in the last fifty. Infotech will bring many positive changes, making some jobs more rewarding and challenging. At the same time, there will be job loss in some areas, as well as boredom and depersonalization.[1]

Technology will bring to our children's careers changes so vast that they are almost impossible to anticipate. One can approach this rapid acceleration of change from a positive or negative stance. In either case, this change has made itself felt in economic conditions. Some economists suggest that a vast change, a third revolution, is occurring in our economy. (The first was the Agricultural Revolution, about eight thousand years ago, when humans settled in one place, planting crops and domesticating animals. The second was the Industrial Revolution, about two hundred years ago, when machines were added to human and animal labor.)

While the Industrial Revolution enhanced human energy, in many instances, this new revolution *replaces* human energy. This infotech revolution has vast job implications. For example, manufacturers have increased their output by more than 400 percent since 1947, with only a 17 percent increase in personnel. These trends are in a state of rapid change. Ultimate influences on the size of the work force remain to be seen.

There are other economic changes as well. At one time, industry research and development allowed four to eight years for new-product development. Now, many look at a cycle of half that duration. Products now new to the market may have a potential lifespan of one or two years. Previously, the product lifespan was expected to be two to four years.

Manufacturing is no longer local or national, but global. Consider the history of one company. Isaac Singer began making sewing machines in the United States in 1851. By 1970, the Singer Company had expanded to include aerospace electronics. In 1986, the sewing division was spun off and now is an independent company, SSMC. Where are SSMC's sewing machines manufactured? An independent company in Cleveland makes the shells. The motors are made in Campinas, Brazil. The drive shafts come from Monza, Italy. They are assembled in Taiwan and sold worldwide! This small example in the economic picture represents and forecasts similar changes in many companies.

Population growth, the location of that growth, and the age distribution are also sources of change. Significant factors include the increasing number of people age fifty-five and over, the maturing of the baby boomers, the occurrence of the "baby bust," and the decreasing number of people between ages sixteen and twenty-four.

There will be a growing need to find ways to match workers with jobs. Our society needs to discover ways to eliminate the problems of high unemployment and worker scarcity occurring at the same time.

Then there are profound changes in lifestyles. What caused these rapid and drastic changes? an economic need for two incomes per family? the entrance of women into the work force in large numbers? the advent of computer and related technologies? All of these and more contributed to our diverging styles both in the personal and working realms.

The concepts of "where" and "when" in relationship to work and leisure are also changing. The "eight to five" day is now only one possible work schedule. Permanent part-time, flex-time, and temporary full- or part-time are other possibilities. There is a growth in the number of temporary workers. Some nurses and other medical persons can now elect a work week that consists of three twelve-hour days. Throw in sabbaticals, family leave, educational leave, and shared time. Some workers experience a shorter work week, thirty to thirty-five hours, which can allow more time for family, recreation, community service, and education. Others find work schedules even more demanding than in the past. Some take a second job in their new extra "leisure" time.

As the hours change, so does the location of work. "Going to" work is only one of several possibilities. Others include home-based or "cottage" enterprises, often working at home via computers. Many service and sales workers operate best out of a car or van. Indeed, if it is equipped with modular phone, laptop computer, fax, and modem, it may serve as their only office—flexible and mobile. Other workers experience some combination of working at home and going to the office. Growing numbers seem to be self-employed, providing a needed service out of the home. Also increasing are the possibilities for working abroad. In this generation, some may even work in outer space.

PROJECTIONS

As we attempt some projections, we first look at the big picture. The U.S. Bureau of Labor Statistics uses consistent terms to describe the broad classifications of industry and occupations. We will use these terms in the paragraphs that follow. They divide all the employment in our nation into three groups:

1. Service-producing industries (including banking, insurance, health care, education, data processing, and management counseling)
2. Goods-producing industries (including construction, manufacturing of both durable and nondurable goods, and mining)
3. Farming

In the United States in the year 1900, this is how jobs were divided, in round figures: service-producing industries, 30 percent; goods-producing industries, 30 percent; farming, 40 percent. In the year 1970, by contrast, this is how the jobs were divided: service-producing industries, 60 percent; goods-producing industries, 35 percent; farming, 5 percent! One sector of our economy grew dramatically; another shrunk drastically; the third grew modestly, but would soon begin a slow decline. All of these trends will continue, so that the broad distribution of employment opportunities will be different still by the year 2005. Quite likely this is how the jobs will be divided: service-producing industries, 80 percent; goods-producing industries, 18 percent; farming, 2 percent!

Beyond that broad picture, what can our children anticipate about career opportunity? That is very difficult to predict with any precision. As a matter of fact, Carl Daniels, in *The Changing Workplace,* describes three possible scenarios for change in the workplace.[2]

One scenario is quite hopeful of a workplace quite different from today's but filled with opportunity. There is a coming work culture in which the long-term employees will be a small group, connected to the core tasks of the business or organization. The many other tasks will be done by what Charles Handy calls "portfolio people," short-term employees who have a skill, a particular knowledge, an expertise in a body of information, a creative ability or the gift to call it forth from others. These persons may have a number of clients for whom they work part-time. Or they may traverse the country or world, finding opportunities to apply their gifts. The temporary or short-term employee is a growing part of the work force on every level of skill and expertise.[3]

Optimists say that in such a rapidly changing society, there will always be opportunity for the persons who "re-invent themselves, by hook or by crook, every few years at the most. Obsolescence is now the concern—obsession, if he or she is smart—of every person."[4]

In his book, *Odyssey,* former Apple chief John Sculley called forth a new different kind of loyalty. He doesn't expect employees to spend their lives at Apple and can't promise lifetime jobs. He does promise a matchless learning experience for the six months or six years an employee is there—an experience that will make that person more competitive in the next job search. In turn, he asks for passionate support to the company's vision during the stay of employment.

For such a future to come about, Tom Peters sees a challenge to the curious person in a curious society. He points out that the workplace not only needs "information intensification" but "creation intensification"—imagination and curiosity.[5] The person who learns, grows, and develops creative gifts to reinvent the self and the organization—that person will always have an opportunity, say advocates of this scenario.

Carl Daniels describes a second scenario—a "gloom and doom" picture of the future of the workplace. Persons with this view note the shift away from manufacturing, which offered well-paying jobs to many in the past. There is a trend among present employers to downscale jobs on all levels. Unemployment continues to be high, and there is a dwindling middle class. New college graduates have more difficulty finding fitting work than did their counterparts in previous generations.

Persons who look at these matters in this way conclude that the future looks grim. Folks should expect to be underemployed or unemployed. Most new jobs are both low-skilled and low-paying. Levels of middle management are being wiped out. Increasingly, there is a two-tiered work force, and most openings are on the bottom tier.

The third scenario that Carl Daniels considers is the middle road between these two extremes. This is the scenario provided by the U.S. Bureau of Labor Statistics in the *Occupational Outlook Handbook*. They update their forecasts every few years, based on discerned population and other trends. Their projection is much more detailed, and so we shall report it in some detail.

The Bureau of Labor Statistics projects that in the years 1994 to 2005, our nation's industrial profile will change radically. Employment will increase from 121.1 million in 1992 to 147.5 million in 2005, an increase of about 22 percent. Some areas will have faster-than-average growth, some less. This is how it may appear from 1994 to 2005:

Service-producing Industries

Services. In this area, employment is expected to rise 40 percent from 38.6 to 54.2 million, the fastest growing industry division. Job growth in legal services and business services will be rapid. Employment in health services will also make impressive gains.

Retail and Wholesale Trade. Employment in this area is expected to rise by 22 percent. It will increase from 19.3 million to 23.8 million in retail and from 6 to 7.2 million in wholesale. More than half of the new retail jobs will be in eating and drinking places. Grocery stores, department stores, and miscellaneous shopping good stores will also experience increase.

Finance, Insurance, and Real Estate. Anticipated employment increase is 21 percent, from 5.2 to 6.6 million jobs.

Government. Employment in this division is expected to increase by 10 percent from 9.5 to 10.5 million jobs. Most of the growth will be in state and local government. (Public education and public hospitals are not included in this category)

Transportation, Communications, and Public Utilities. Employment is expected to increase 14 percent, making it and government the slowest growing of the service producing industries. However, opportunities in transportation, particularly in trucking and airline transportation services will be better. Opportunities there will grow at about twice the rate of the rest of the industries in this division.

Goods-producing Industries

Construction. This is the only goods-producing division that is expected to show an increase in employment. It will be up 26 percent from 4.5 to 5.6 million jobs.

Manufacturing. Employment will decrease from 18 to 17.5 million jobs—a decline of 3 percent. Job losses are expected to be greatest in the steel, aircraft, apparel, weaving, finishing, yarn, and thread industries. There will be some increase in job opportunities in firms producing electronics, computing equipment, medical instruments and supplies, plastics, commercial printing, and business forms.

Mining. Employment will probably decline from 631 to 562 thousand, a 11 percent drop.

Agriculture, Forestry, and Fishing. After declining for many decades, there is an anticipated small growth projected. There will be growth in agricultural services, but continued decline in crops, livestock, and livestock products. There is an anticipated loss of 500,000 self employed persons from family farms.

We now turn to forecasts regarding occupational profile. In the following section, we will begin with the occupational areas in which the greatest growth is anticipated and list them in descending order.

Professional specialty occupations will grow the fastest, 37 percent, from 16.6 to 22.8 million jobs. Human services workers, computer scientists, systems analysts, physical therapists, special education teachers, and operations research analysts are some of the fastest growing opportunities in this group.

Service occupations will grow by 33 percent from 19.4 to 25.8 million. Some of the fastest growth will be among homemaker-home health aides, nursing aids, child care workers, guard, and correction officers.

Technicians and related support occupations will grow at a rate of 32 percent from 4.3 to 5.7 million. Paralegal, health technicians and technologists such as licensed practical nurses and radiological technologists will add large numbers of jobs.

Executive, administrative and managerial occupations will increase by 26 percent from 21.1 to 25.2 million. Familiarity with computers will continue to be important to a growing number of workers in this area.

Transportation and material moving occupations will increase by 22 percent from 4.7 to 5.7 million. Bus drivers and truck drivers will be among the occupations with growth.

Marketing and sales occupations will increase by 21 percent from 13 to 15.7 million. This is about the average growth anticipated in these years. Travel agents, services sales representatives, securities and financial services sales workers, and real estate appraisers will experience faster than average growth.

Helpers, laborers, and material movers will increase by 17 percent, less than average growth—from 4.5 to 5.2 million. Workers in this group perform routine unskilled tasks, assisting skilled workers. Some of these routine tasks will become increasingly automated.

Mechanics, installers, and repairers—those who adjust, maintain, and repair automobiles, industrial equipment, computers, and other types of equipment—will grow by 15 percent from 4.8 to 5.6 million.

Administrative support occupations, including clerical will grow by 14 percent from 22.3 to 25.4 million. Technological advances will probably slow employment growth for stenographers, typists, and word processors.

Agriculture, forestry, fishing and related occupations will have only a 3 percent increase from 3.5 to 3.6 million. While demand for food, fiber, and wood will increase with the world's population, the use of more productive farming and forestry methods and consolidation of smaller farms will limit opportunity.

Production occupations—who set up, install, adjust, operate, and tend machinery and equipment—will have little change from their 1992 level of 12.2 million.[6]

No one quite knows which of these three scenarios will be most accurate for the overall employment picture. There simply is no stable, predictable "job market." What is known is that individual jobs will undergo vast change. Infotech will impact many types of jobs, including proofreaders, billing clerks, library assistants, keypunchers, mail carriers, filing clerks, telegraph operators, plateprinters, drafters, machinists, secretaries, mechanics, and sales clerks.

An example of changes already occurring can be seen in the modern office. Here the use of word processing and electronic information storage is eliminating many filing and routine clerical jobs. It is also redefining the content of the secretaries' activities.

There will also be the development of new occupations as a result of some of the changes we have discussed. High-tech industries will need a broad spectrum of engineers and technicians. S. Norman Feingold and Maxine H. Atwater suggest a list of nineteen new occupations, some of which already exist and some of which have yet to come on-line:

1. artificial intelligence technician
2. aquaculturist
3. automotive fuel cell battery technician
4. bionic electron technician
5. computational linguist
6. cryonics technician
7. electronic mail technician
8. fiber optic technician
9. fusion engineer
10. hazardous waste technician
11. information broker
12. leisure consultant
13. medical diagnostic imaging technician
14. relocation counselor
15. robot technician
16. software club director
17. space mechanic
18. underwater archeologist
19. water quality specialist[7]

The space program is an area where many new occupations are developing. Areas of specialization include:

Aeronautical flight research
Airborne science
Planetary spacecraft development
Design and fabrication of space equipment
Space transportation passenger selection criteria

FUTURE WORK CHALLENGES

We now shift our approach to speak of the heart, of passions, of challenges. God may cry out to your child and summon participation to seek solutions to the challenges we meet as a nation, culture, and world. Perhaps your child will want to tackle some of our currently identified challenges.

Challenge—Education: Our entire educational system needs attention, from the public school system to technical and/or trade schools and four year colleges. On-the-job-training and continuing education will be offered throughout the our lifetimes. Education will play an increasingly dominant role in our lives. Some estimate that the average worker will spend one out of every ten years retraining!

In order to achieve education's necessary tasks, the tools of technology must become the tools of education. This includes making the technologies of closed-circuit TV, computers, laser discs, and videocassettes into tools of the classroom. However, there will still need to be a personal element in education. Persons and technologies are needed to fill the gap between our undereducated population and our sophisticated, technical society. Will this be the challenge to which your child responds?

Challenge—Environment: Longstanding and yet unanswered questions are those dealing with acid rain, fluorocarbons, and toxic wastes. Pollution of all kinds—noise, air, water—continues as a plague. Solutions will come with the cooperation of botanists, zoologists, meteorologists, hydrologists, chemists, engineers, and economists.

Challenge—Waste Materials: "How can we trash the trash?" The need for new and economical methods of dealing with the 3.5 pounds of garbage each of us creates daily is clear. The field of bioconversion will need planners, economists, engineers, chemists, and innovation and creativity.

Challenge—Health Care: This field will expand and encompass possibilities ranging from research for dramatic new cures to the administration of home health care programs. Like many fields, health care will also face the need to balance the mix of professionals within its domain. With the increasing importance of health maintenance organizations, home health care, and retirement facilities, the health care industry will face new challenges. Among these are employing persons in a variety of occupations, such as administration and management, retirement facility planning, etc. All of these are occupations that previously had not existed in this field. There will be an increased demand for supportive professions, such as physical and occupational therapists and social workers.

At the same time, research by the Graduate Medical Education National Advisory Committee is predicting a possible "doctor glut" in the future. One can conclude that challenge and growth in health care will continue, but the mix of professionals within the field will change.

Challenge—Religious and Social Services: This is a family of careers that will hold lively opportunities over future decades.

Holistic health and treatment will increasingly become concerns for all, and thus for mental health professionals who serve the public. Studies in strong families and in family systems theory may open doors for some. They may engage in careers that are devoted to reversing family decay and enabling affirmative family life. Stress management, play therapy, and humor therapy may grow in influence. Flexibility and instability in the job market may create the need for more career counselors. The changes of tomorrow will bring pressures upon persons who, in turn, will need the assistance of the caring professions.

Churches and synagogues will need gifted leaders as well. Thinkers will need to create theologies that relate to the secular discoveries of new ages. Artists, writers, and journalists will need to communicate faith options in such an age. Local churches will need not only clergy but also specialists in serving a wide variety of needs. Children, youth, families, singles, the bereaved, divorced persons, the disenfranchised—each of these groups needs gifted leaders.

There is yet another factor to mention in regard to opportunities in church vocations. A large number of persons entered church vocations following World War II, many of whom have already retired or soon will do so. Several major denominations estimate that 35 percent of their ministers and missionaries will retire in the next ten years! The Roman Catholic church is experiencing an even more severe shortage. A wide variety of opportunities for priests, nuns, and lay religious leaders are opening up in Catholic parishes.

Challenge—Politics and Political Science: Governments on local, county, state, and national levels will continue to be huge employers. Each age will have its political leaders. They, in turn, will have staffs and departments executing the programs and policies of government. What kinds of people will occupy those offices and tasks? Do we not all long for political leaders with the virtues of personal faith and integrity?

We need leaders with vision broad enough to develop new approaches to the challenges of new ages.

We have been talking about projections to help our children prepare to make choices. Because of the rapid changes that are occurring in our world, anticipating the future is essential. Only by knowing the possibilities and being aware of the alternatives can we be prepared to make fitting choices.

How to Anticipate

How can you help your child anticipate the future? Jim O'Toole, in an article titled "How to Forecast Your Own Working Future," suggests that we can use the tools of the futurist to do our own forecasting.[8]

However, he cautions about two frequent errors of forecasting. The first is to assume that the future will be a continuation of current trends. This approach is wrong because it does not take into consideration the unexpected, the surprises the future inevitably presents. The second error is to anticipate only one outcome. This is a failure to recognize the possibility of many alternatives.

Encourage your child to develop scenarios concerning the future by listing a number of possible futures. Base these scenarios on a unifying theme, such as an interest in a particular field or using a special skill. Then ask, "What conditions would lead to these varying futures?" To increase the validity of the forecasts, identify the elements of continuity, change and choice that could influence their outcome.

Continuity: Ask, "What present trends could have an impact on this possible future event?" What in the past and current environment will continue into the future? If you are focusing on careers, look for trends that provide opportunities to be innovative, to seek new solutions. Is the trend strong enough to endure or merely a fad? What in your personal situation do you want to continue?

Change: Unexpected events that break into the chain of continuity are the most likely to disrupt forecasts. These could include: economic considerations such as depression, inflation, or changes in governmental priorities; new social concerns and movements, such as the civil rights and antiwar movement in the recent past; and more personal events, such as job loss, illness, graduation from high school. There are also deliberate, planned changes to consider, plan for, and create. These might include moving to increase the availability of certain jobs and obtaining the necessary education or experience.

Choice: This is an area in which the individual's personality type comes into play. Ask your child to consider the question, "What would be the most important feature of an ideal job?" Or to put it another way, "Where does my unique interest and gifts fit in this emerging world?"

Encourage intentionality in your child's decisions. Too often, our society succumbs to "fads" in occupations as in other areas. For example, there may be occupations with great opportunities, such as computer scientist or electrical engineer. However, an intuitive/feeling person would probably be quite miserable in either of those occupations. Tomorrow's world of work will be like today's in this regard. The opportunities will be varied enough for a person to find a close fit. However, this will require self-knowledge and the willingness to make choices that arise from within the individual.

QUESTIONS AND ANSWERS

Question: This topic is overwhelming. You describe such far-ranging change and so much uncertainty. Are there any topics on this subject about which I can be certain?

Answer: There is at least one—the need for education and preparedness. We see this theme repeated in numerous ways. The *Occupational Outlook Handbook* stated that "the fastest growing occupations will be those that require the most educational preparation."[9] The unskilled and low-skilled job market is shrinking as automation, robots, and other technology take the workers' places. The future job market and the competition from other workers strongly indicate the need for educational preparedness.

What kind of education should a person seek? Two kinds: On the one hand, one needs broad-based education. It is good to know the overview of a field, the basic comprehension that translates from one job to another. On the other hand, increasing numbers will need technological skills, including knowledge of how to operate, repair, and improve the many devices in today's workplace. Some have termed the coming ten years "the decade of the technician." Even those aspiring to manage will be well advised to have some technical know-how.

In addition to that, we hope for education that expands the mind, broadens one's appreciation of the arts, and stimulates the growth of the spirit. There is a lot to be said for a liberal arts education, whether it leads to a career or not.

Question: How can today's young person possibly select and prepare for a career in a future that holds this much change and uncertainty?

Answer: A young person doesn't have to plan his or her whole career—only to select, as wisely as possible, where to start. Some years ago, a U.S. Labor Department report stated that the person entering the work force could be expected to change jobs six or seven times on the average. Quite probably this number is growing. These changes may be within a "career trajectory"—that is, a variety of jobs with increasing complexity and responsibility within one career area. Or these changes may be complete changes from one career area to another.

One need not apologize for such changes; they will occur frequently. The job market might impose these changes upon a person, or they may reflect an individual's new interests and preferences.

The question, therefore for a young person contemplating the future need not be, "What do I want to do with my life?" Rather, it can be, "What do I want to do for the next several years? Where would I like to start?"

Question: It's often difficult for the recent graduate to find that first job. Is there any wisdom in all this for the new job seeker?

Answer: This topic has been researched by Robert O. Snelling Sr. and Anne M. Snelling.[10] They suggest that if the new worker picks a field that is experiencing growth and knows the most frequent entry-level jobs in that field, a good future beckons. They spell this out by describing "The Top Seven Entry-level Job Areas." Here, in brief, is their perception of the areas and the most likely entry-level jobs:

1. *Computers:* "We're in the midst of a computer explosion, and job growth in the field is destined to be superb. What's more, computer expertise can lead to employment in fields as diverse as health services, scientific research, retailing, and finance." Entry-level jobs are: computer service technician, who maintains and repairs the computers; and systems analyst, who designs and tests computer programs created to pinpoint and solve specific problems.
2. *Engineering:* "A degree in engineering is once again a golden passport to an excellent career."[11] They suggest investigating the specialties of biomedical, chemical, and electrical engineering for particularly fruitful possibilities.
3. *Finance:* Entry-level positions to seek include: junior analyst, security sales representative, banking trainee, claims representative, and accountant.
4. *Health services and technology:* Beginning workers are particularly needed for these positions: nurse, physical therapist, electrocardiograph technician, emergency medical technician, and radiologic (X-ray) technologist.
5. *Marketing:* Opportunities for beginners may be: junior copywriter, junior analyst, and public relations assistant.
6. *Media and communications:* Places to start may include: *broadcast technician* or *news assistant.*
7. *Sales:* "The sales field is hot and getting hotter."[12] Entry-level jobs include: advertising sales representative, computer sales representative, direct sales representative, food sales representative, manufacturers' sales representative, and insurance agent.

Of course, if nothing on this list fits your recent graduate, she or he will have to look a little harder in those places where, perhaps, others are not looking.

Question: This chapter is mind-boggling, particularly in an attempt to apply a belief in Christian vocation. What the Bible said about "call" and "vocation" was written in much simpler, pastoral times. Do those teachings apply today?

Answer: We believe so. Certainly, all the complex technology has not gone beyond the mind of our Creator God! Nor does God care any less for people and their needs simply because there are more people in more complicated urban settings. God calls each of us to responsible stewardship of our gifts and our times.

Epilogue

A Final Word

Though there are thousands of job descriptions in our complex society, a Christian understanding of vocation comes down to a few simple, basic considerations. Roy Lewis suggests that a person discerns vocation in any opportunity by asking these four questions:

1. Can I serve God in this vocation?
2. Can I serve my neighbor in this vocation?
3. Is this vocation in harmony with my faith?
4. Will this vocation use and enhance my natural abilities?[1]

Richard Bolles suggests that each person has a threefold mission in life. The first two are shared with all people: "(1) to seek to stand hour by hour in the conscious presence of God, the One from whom your Mission is derived; . . . (2) to do what you can, moment by moment, day by day, step by step, to make this world a better place, following the leading and guidance of God's Spirit within you and around you."[2]

In Bolles's view, one's third mission is uniquely one's own, and that is:

a. to exercise that Talent which you particularly came to Earth to use—your greatest gift, which you most delight to use,
b. in the place(s) or setting(s) which God has caused to appeal to you the most,
c. and for those purposes which God most needs to have done in the world.[3]

To be willing to ask those questions and to live with those aspirations is to live vocationally.

But what is the parent's place in all this? A long time ago, the authors of this book began a search to discover the answer to that very question: How can parents be vocational resource persons to their children? What we found out is that there are no mysterious, magical answers. Rather, there are a trillion little discoveries, a million small decisions, thousands of human interactions, and hundreds of skills, which all come together for each person in a unique way.

As a parent and child work together on the gift that is that child's life, they don't know the outcome. Perhaps it will be quite different from what they expected. But with the vision that only fathers and mothers possess, parents recognize the joy of the search and the beauty of the discovery. Parents may even discover that they have been used by God to help their children discover their call, their vocation.

Appendix

How to Benefit from a Visit to a College or University

Every youth-parent team will develop its own style of campus visit and assessment. The following paragraphs offer a few suggestions to help get started.

Both youth and parent should have studied the printed materials (as mentioned in chapter 5). They should have concluded that the school at least merits a look. However, it is quite all right to do a "trial run" at a nearby college, just for the practice. Some persons have even found a school they liked that way.

Make an appointment for a visit. Preferably, this should be during the week when regular activities are going on.

Very likely a person will be assigned to show you around. This person's job is to help you see the school in its best light. That is okay, but you should add a touch of realism to this tour. In addition to the nice new dormitory your guide will show you, ask to see the ones usually assigned incoming freshmen. In addition to whatever showpiece facilities your guide shows you, see the facilities in areas where your child has an interest. Ask to see a list of classes. Request the chance to visit randomly a class or two of your child's or your choice. Note: Is the instructor prepared? Is the instructor a professor or a teaching assistant? Is there attention, dialogue, participation, attendance by students? Is this class an engaging learning environment?

Visit the library. Is it well cared for? adequately supplied? Wander the stacks to look for resources in some given area in which you feel

181

well informed. Does the library include basic works? Does it seem to be up to date? Is there an atmosphere of study and inquiry?

There are two levels of inquiry here. On the first level, you and your child are trying to discover the school that offers competent departments your child may choose to pursue. But on the second level, you are seeking an intuitive sense of comfort, community, fit. Your child will probably grow more aware of this with succeeding visits.

Here are a few examples: While I inspected labs, libraries, and classes, my children looked at other things. One daughter once rejected a school because of the size of the parking lot. She quickly picked up that the school we were visiting was largely a commuter school. She was hoping for more of a sense of community with her fellow students. Another daughter sensed that a school was largely attended by upper-middle-class students. She had gone to high school with classmates that had more than she, and she didn't want that same experience in college. And so she wisely rejected a very good school.

Another potential source of comfort or discomfort is the size of a school. One student may want a small community where he or she can be known and participate in a variety of school activities. Another may desire a large school with lots of people who share his or her interests and potential major.

Attention to bulletin boards (for range of activities) and how people dress (could I be comfortable here?) may be important. So may visits with the persons in the student union or other places on campus. Sometimes the students with whom we visited gave a better impression of the school than the paid guide. At other times they gave a worse impression, but they filled in the picture. Always we found students helpful and informative.

My children generally wanted to go to the bookstore—to buy a T-shirt or sweatshirt. This was true whether they were seriously considering the school or not. They tell me that the style is to wear sweatshirts from every school except the one you actually attend!

Parents and children may want to make some of these initial visits together. However, in time, there is real wisdom in the students' making some of these visits on their own. Perhaps they can visit a sibling, cousin, or friend from their religious community or high school on the campus of interest. This can add to the young person's sense of owner-ship of this decision.

Eventually, the visit will be only one factor in choosing a school. There will also be the insights from written material, costs, and finan-cial aid packages.

If possible, keep college selection—including the campus visit—in perspective. One of my daughters liked most of the schools she visited and was hard-pressed to make a selection. I tried to console her with the advice, "Honey, as far as I can tell, you can't make a bad choice from your list." Still, it was difficult for her to reduce that list to four and then to one. A year or two later, after visiting with students from several of the schools she considered, she told me, "Dad, you were right. One of the schools I looked at just didn't have what I needed. Any of the others would have been fine."

On the other hand, it may be perfectly appropriate for a person to transfer from one college to another a time or two. At best, careful col-lege selection increases one's chances of choosing a good fit. But there is a certain amount of guesswork and luck in this choice as well. If the selected school just does not fit the bill, or if the student's needs and in-terests change, a transfer may be the best possible thing to do. The ear-lier searching may help a student "fine-tune" the next selection.

Give yourself as much time as possible. Be prepared for college ex-ploration to be exhausting work. (That's not to deny that it can be fun at the same time.) I remember one day when one of my daughters wanted to take a quick look at some schools near where we then lived. My daughter and I agreed to spend a couple hours on each of two campuses about thirty miles apart. We reached the second campus at about midafternoon on a hot spring day. Both of us were so bushed we could hardly get out of the car. As a result, we drove around the campus and quickly left. For all we know, it could have been the Harvard of the West, but we didn't have the energy to give it a chance. On the other hand, if students have a chance to meet folks, observe, imagine them-selves in that setting—that may be the information on which they can base a good choice.

NOTES

PART I

1. Frederick Buechner, *Listening to Your Life* (San Francisco: Harper San Francisco, 1992), 185–86.

1. The Gift You May Not Know You Have

1. Evelyn Eaton Whitehead and James D. Whitehead, *Seasons of Strength: New Visions of Adult Christian Maturing* (New York: Doubleday, 1984), 23.

2. What the Caring Parent Can Offer

1. Richard Foster, *Money, Sex, and Power* (San Francisco: Harper and Row, 1985), 84.

3. Christian Perspectives on the Vocational Quest

1. Robert C. Leslie, *Jesus and Logotherapy* (Nashville: Abingdon Press, 1965), 37.

2. Whitehead and Whitehead, 9.

3. James W. Fowler, *Becoming Adult, Becoming Christian* (San Francisco: Harper and Row, 1984), 93.

4. Ibid.

5. Elton Trueblood, *The Common Ventures of Life* (New York: Harper and Brothers, 1949), 87.

6. Fowler, 95.

7. Ibid., 96.

8. Bruce Larson, *Believe and Belong* (Old Tappan, N.J.: Fleming H. Revell Company, 1982), 56.

9. William A. Overholt, "Choosing a Life-Work in a Changing World" (mimeographed).

10. Roy W. Fairchild, *The Waiting Game* (Camden, N.J.: Thomas Nelson, 1971), 43.

11. Richard P. Olson, *A Job or a Vocation?* (Nashville: Thomas Nelson, 1973), 35–43, 92–93.

12. Viktor E. Frankl, *The Doctor and the Soul* (New York: Alfred A. Knopf, 1966), 61.

13. Roy Lewis, *Choosing Your Career, Finding Your Vocation* (New York: Paulist Press, 1989), 56.

14. Ibid., 57.

15. Fowler, 103–5.

16. A friend told me this story. I regret that I do not know the source.

PART II

1. Whitehead and Whitehead, 10, 23.

4. Early Childhood

1. Barbara M. Newman and Philip R. Newman, *Development through Life: A Psychosocial Approach* (Homewood, Ill.: The Dorsey Press, 1979), 18–19.

2. Ibid., 111–13.

3. Ibid., 124.

4. Ibid., 133.

5. Ibid., 136.

6. Ibid., 138.

7. Gary Landreth, "Rules of Thumb for Rearing Responsible Children" (paper presented at the Winter Workshop of the Christian Preschool Association, Prairie Village, Kans., Jan. 1987).

8. Robert Fulghum, *All I Really Needed to Know I Learned in Kindergarten* (New York: Ivy Books, 1986).

9. Jean Curtis, *Working Mothers* (Garden City, N.Y.: Doubleday and Company, 1976).

10. Patsy Blalock (Conversation with author, Prairie Village, Kans., Feb. 1994).

5. Childhood in the School Years

1. Mary Schramm, *Gifts of Grace* (Minneapolis: Augsburg, 1982), 51–53.

2. Leo F. Buscaglia, *Love* (New York: Fawcett Crest Books, 1972), 22–23.

3. Newman and Newman, 179.

4. Ibid., 178.

5. Ibid., 189.

6. Ibid.

7. Ibid., 191.

8. Ibid., 230.

9. David Keirsey and Marilyn Bates, *Please Understand Me* (Del Mar, Calif.: Prometheus Nemesis Book Company, 1984), 100.

10. Newman and Newman, 260.

11. Gordon Lawrence, *People Types and Tiger Stripes: A Practical Guide to Learning Styles* (Gainesville, Fla.: Center for Applications of Psychological Type, 1979), 40.

12. Budd Schulberg, "My Wonderful Lousy Poem," *Family Weekly,* Oct. 11, 1964, 67–69.

6. Youth in the Middle-High and Senior-High Years

1. Newman and Newman, 272.

2. Ibid., 275.

3. Ibid., 283.

4. Ibid., 285.

5. Donald E. Super and Martin J. Bohn Jr., *Occupational Psychology* (Belmont, Calif.: Wadsworth, 1970), 136–48.

6. Ibid., 148.

7. Luther B. Otto, *How to Help Your Child Choose a Career* (New York: M. Evans and Company, 1984), 240.

8. Charlotte Lobb, *Exploring Apprenticeship Careers* (New York: Richards Rosen Press, 1978), 17–27.

9. Ibid.

10. Michael J. McManus, *Marriage Savers* (Grand Rapids, Mich.: Zondervan Publishing House, 1993), 64.

11. Alan Guttmacher, *Eleven Million Teenagers: What Can Be Done about the Epidemic of Adolescent Pregnancies in the United States?* (New York: Guttmacher Institute, 1976), 18.

12. Fred M. Hechinger, *Fateful Choices: Healthy Youth for the Twenty-first Century* (New York: Hill and Wang, a division of Farrar, Straus, and Giroux, 1992).

13. John Westerhoff III, *Will Our Children Have Faith?* (New York: Seabury Press, 1976), 96.

14. Ibid., 93–96.

15. Otto, 15.

16. Ibid., 21, 53–60.

17. *The AAUW Report: How Schools Shortchange Girls, Executive Summary* (Washington, D.C.: The AAUW Educational Foundation, 1992), 1–5.

18. Pam Penfold, "Wanted: Women Scientists," *Summit Magazine* (spring 1991): 22.

19. Otto, 241–43.

20. "Myths about College Costs," *Kansas City Star,* May 22, 1988.

7. Moving into Adulthood: From Eighteen to Thirty

1. Daniel J. Levinson et al., *The Seasons of a Man's Life* (New York: Alfred A. Knopf, 1978).

2. Newman and Newman, 319.

3. Ibid., 325.

4. Ibid., 327.

5. Karen Levin Coburn and Madge Lawrence Treeger, *Letting Go: A Parents' Guide to Today's College Experience* (Bethesda, Md.: Adler and Adler Publishers, 1988), 11.

6. Ibid., 128–29.

7. Ibid., 197.

8. Ibid., 231–32.

9. Ibid., 234–35.

10. Ibid., 238.

11. Otto, 204–5.

12. Coburn and Treeger, 124.

13. Otto, 56.

14. Ibid., 58.

15. Ibid.

16. Levinson et al., 52–62.

17. Newman and Newman, 365–66.

18. Otto, 28.

19. Newman and Newman, 372–73.

20. E. Erikson, *Dimensions of a New Identity* (New York: Norton, 1974), 124.

21. David M. Gross and Sophfronia Scott, "Twentysomething," *Time,* July 16, 1990, 57.

22. Ibid., 59–60.

8. Further Ways a Family Can Enrich a Child's Vocational Discovery

1. Larson, 21.

2. Lewis, 17.

3. Ibid., 20.

4. Viktor E. Frankl, *The Will to Meaning* (New York: New American Library, 1969), 69–71.

5. Richard Nelson Bolles, *The Three Boxes of Life* (Berkeley, Calif.: Ten Speed Press, 1978–81).

6. Dean Hummel and Carl McDaniels, *How to Help Your Child Find a Career* (Washington, D.C.: Acropolis Books, 1979), 23–28.

7. Barbara Sher, *Wishcraft: How to Get What You Really Want* (New York: Ballantine Books, 1979), 15–23.

8. Bill Page, "The Difference That Play Makes" (Peterborough, N.H., mimeographed).

9. Ann Kaufman, "Are You a Playful Person?" from "Are These Things Happening in Your Life Right Now?" (Longmont, Colo.: Learnings Unlimited, 1982).

10. David Campbell, *Take the Road to Creativity and Get Off Your Dead End* (Allen, Tex.: Argus Communications, 1977), 84–86.

11. Gordon Porter Miller with Bob Oskam, *Teaching Your Child to Make Decisions* (New York: Harper and Row, 1984), 15–21.

12. Hummel and McDaniels, 37–39.

13. Richard Nelson Bolles, *The 1995 What Color Is Your Parachute?* (Berkeley, Calif.: Ten Speed Press, 1995), 65–66.

14. Mindy Bingham, Judy Edmondson, and Sandy Stryker, *Choices: A Teen Woman's Journal for Self-Awareness and Personal Planning* (Santa Barbara, Calif.: Advocacy Press, 1984).

15. Mindy Bingham, Judy Edmondson, and Sandy Stryker, *Challenges: A Young Man's Journal for Self-Awareness and Personal Planning* (Santa Barbara, Calif.: Advocacy Press, 1984).

16. *Discover* (Iowa City: American College Testing Program, 1994).

17. *Guidance Information System* (Cambridge, Mass.: Houghton Mifflin, The Riverside Publishing Company, 1994).

PART III

1. Whitehead and Whitehead, 10.

9. What the Experts Can Tell Us—Process

1. Donald E. Super et al., *Career Development: Self-Concept Theory* (New York: College Entrance Examination Board, 1963), 1.

2. Ibid., 11–14.

3. Hummel and McDaniels, 19.

4. Bolles, *The Three Boxes of Life,* 142–55.

5. Bolles, *The 1995 What Color Is Your Parachute?* 169 ff..

6. Donald E. Super, *The Psychology of Careers: An Introduction to Vocational Development* (New York: Harper and Brothers, 1957), 241.

7. Richard Nelson Bolles and Victoria Zenoff, *The Beginning Quick Job Hunting Map* (Berkeley, Calif.: Ten Speed Press, 1979).

8. Ibid., 2.

9. Carol Gilligan, *In a Different Voice* (Cambridge, Mass.: Harvard University Press, 1985), 6.

10. Nancy E. Betz and Louise F. Fitzgerald, *The Career Psychology of Women* (Orlando, Fla.: Harcourt, Brace, Jovanovich, Academic Press, 1987), 250.

11. Ibid.

12. Norma Carr-Ruffino, "Women's Barriers and Opportunities." In *The Encyclopedia of Career Change and Work Issues,* ed. Lawrence K. Jones (Phoenix: Oryx Press, 1992), 328–29.

10. What the Psychologists Can Tell Us—Personality

1. John L. Holland, *Making Vocational Choices* (Englewood Cliffs, N.J.: Prentice-Hall, 1985–93); David J. Srebalus, "Vocational Choice: John Holland's Theory," in *The Encyclopedia of Career Change and Work Issues,* ed. Lawrence K. Jones (Phoenix: Oryx Press, 1992), 320; and Bolles, *The 1995 What Color Is Your Parachute,* 168.

2. Holland, *Making Vocational Choices,* 54–59.

3. Ibid., 89–90.

4. Edward K. Strong Jr., *Strong-Campbell Vocational Preference Test* (Stanford: Stanford University Press, 1985).

5. John L. Holland, *The Self Directed Search* (Odessa, Tex.: Psychological Assessment Resource, 1990).

6. Katharine C. Briggs and Isabel Briggs-Myers, *Myers-Briggs Type Indicator* (Palo Alto, Calif.: Consulting Psychologists Press, 1987).

7. Keirsey and Bates, 22.

8. Ibid., 101.

9. Ibid.

10. Isabel Briggs-Myers and Peter B. Myers, *Gifts Differing* (Palo Alto, Calif.: Consulting Psychologists Press, 1980).

11. Ibid., 159.

11. Significant Employment Trends

1. Andy Hines, "Jobs and Infotech—Work in the Information Society," *The Futurist* (Jan.–Feb. 1994), 9.

2. Carl McDaniels, *The Changing Workplace: Career Counseling Strategies For the 1990's and Beyond* (San Francisco: Bass Publishers, 1989).

3. Charles Handy, "The Coming Work Culture," *Lear's* (Jan. 1991), 54, 60.

4. Tom Peters, "Re-inventing Civilization," *Future Outlook 94/95* (Bethesda, Md.: World Future Society, 1994).

5. Ibid., 17.

6. U.S. Department of Labor, Bureau of Labor Statistics, *Occupational Outlook Handbook* (April 1994), 15–16.

7. S. Norman Feingold and Maxine H. Atwater, *New Emerging Careers: Today, Tomorrow, and in the 21st Century* (Garrett Park, Md.: Garrett Park Press, 1988), 82.

8. James O'Toole, "How to Forecast Your Own Working Future," in *Careers Tomorrow*, ed. Edward Cornish (Bethesda, Md.: World Future Society, 1983), 19, 25.

9. U.S. Department of Labor, *Occupational Outlook Handbook*, 12.

10. Robert O. Snelling Sr. and Anne M. Snelling, *Jobs! What They Are . . . Where They Are . . . What They Pay* (New York: Simon and Schuster, 1989), 24.

11. Ibid.

12. Ibid., 23–27.

Epilogue

1. Lewis, 84.

2. Richard Nelson Bolles, *How to Find Your Mission in Life* (Berkeley, Calif.: Ten Speed Press, 1991), 12–13.

3. Ibid., 14.

BIBLIOGRAPHY

AAUW Report, The: How Schools Shortchange Girls, Executive Summary. Washington, D.C.: The AAUW Educational Foundation, 1992.

America's Top 300 Jobs. Minneapolis, Minn.: JIST Works, 1990.

Betz, Nancy E., and Louise F. Fitzgerald. *The Career Psychology of Women.* Orlando, Fla.: Harcourt, Brace, Jovanovich, Academic Press, 1987.

Bingham, Mindy, Judy Edmondson, and Sandy Stryker. *Challenges: A Young Man's Journal for Self-Awareness and Personal Planning.* Santa Barbara, Calif.: Advocacy Press, 1984.

————. *Choices: A Teen Woman's Journal for Self-Awareness and Personal Planning.* Santa Barbara, Calif.: Advocacy Press, 1984.

Blalock, Patsy. Conversation with Author, Prairie Village, Kans., Feb. 1994.

Bolles, Richard Nelson. *How to Find Your Mission in Life.* Berkeley, Calif.: Ten Speed Press, 1991.

————. *The New Quick Job-Hunting Map: How to Create a Picture of Your Ideal Job or Next Career.* Berkeley, Calif.: Ten Speed Press, 1990.

————. *The 1995 What Color Is Your Parachute?* Berkeley, Calif.: Ten Speed Press, 1995.

————. *The Three Boxes of Life.* Berkeley, Calif.: Ten Speed, 1978–81.

Bolles, Richard Nelson, and Victoria Zenoff. *The Beginning Quick Job Hunting Map.* Berkeley, Calif.: Ten Speed Press, 1979.

Briggs, Katharine C., and Isabel Briggs Myers. *Myers-Briggs Type Indicator.* Palo Alto, Calif.: Consulting Psychologists Press, 1987.

Buechner, Frederick. *Listening to Your Life.* San Francisco: Harper San Francisco, 1992.

Buscaglia, Leo F. *Love.* New York: Fawcett Crest Books, 1972.

Campbell, David. *Take the Road to Creativity and Get Off Your Dead End.* Allen, Tex.: Argus Communications, 1977.

Carr-Ruffino, Norma. "Women's Barrier's and Opportunities." In *The Encyclopedia of Career Change and Work Issues,* edited by Lawrence K. Jones. Phoenix: Oryx Press, 1992.

Chapman, Lawrence. "Tomorrow's Global Economy." *The Futurist,* July-Aug. 1987, 26, 27.

Charland, William A., Jr. *Life-Work: Meaningful Employment in an Age of Limits.* New York: Continuum, 1986.

Clemes, Harris, and Reynold Bean. *Self-Esteem: The Key to Your Child's Well-Being.* New York: G. P. Putnam's Sons, 1981.

Coburn, Karen Levin, and Madge Lawrence Treeger. *Letting Go: A Parents' Guide to Today's College Experience.* Bethesda, Md.: Adler and Adler, 1988.

Colorado Divison of Employment and Training, Colorado Department of Labor and Employment. *Occupational Employment Outlook, 1985-1990.* Denver, 1991.

Cornish, Edward, ed. *Careers Tomorrow: The Outlook for Work in a Changing World.* Bethesda, Md.: World Future Society, 1983.

Cotham, James C., III. *Career Shock.* Brentwood, Tenn.: JM Productions, 1988.

Curran, Dolores. *Traits of a Healthy Family.* New York: Ballantine Books, 1983.

Curtis, Jean. *Working Mothers.* Garden City, N.Y.: Doubleday, 1976.

Diehl, William E. *Thank God, It's Monday!* Philadelphia: Fortress Press, 1982.

Discover. Iowa City: American College Testing Program, 1994.

Drucker, Peter F. "A Growing Mismatch of Jobs and Job Seekers." *The Wall Street Journal,* March 26, 1985.

Erikson, E. *Dimensions of a New Identity.* New York: Norton, 1974.

Evely, Louis. *Training Children for Maturity.* Westminster, Md.: Newman Press, 1968.

Fairchild, Roy W. *The Waiting Game.* Camden, N.J.: Thomas Nelson Inc., 1971.

Feingold, S. Norman, and Maxine H. Atwater. *New Emerging Careers: Today, Tomorrow, and in the 21st Century.* Garrett Park, Md.: Garrett Park Press, 1988.

Foster, Richard. *Money, Sex, and Power.* San Francisco: Harper and Row, 1985.

Fowler, James W. *Becoming Adult, Becoming Christian.* San Francisco: Harper and Row, 1984.

Frankl, Viktor E. *The Doctor and the Soul.* New York: Alfred A. Knopf, 1966.

———. *Man's Search for Meaning.* New York: Washington Square Press, Inc., 1959.

————. *The Will to Meaning.* New York: New American Library, 1969.

Fulghum, Robert. *All I Really Needed to Know I Learned in Kindergarten.* New York: Ivy Books, 1986, 1988.

Gates, Anita. *90 Most Promising Careers for the 80s.* New York: Monarch Press, 1982.

Gilligan, Carol. *In a Different Voice.* Cambridge: Harvard University Press, 1985.

Gould, Shirley. *How to Raise an Independent Child.* New York: St. Martin's Press, 1979.

Gross, David M., and Sophfronia Scott. "Twentysomething." *Time,* July 16, 1990, 57–62.

Guidance Information System. Cambridge, Mass.: Houghton Mifflin, The Riverside Publishing Company, 1994.

Guttmacher, Alan. *Eleven Million Teenagers: What Can Be Done about the Epidemic of Adolescent Pregnancies in the United States?* New York: Guttmacher Institute, 1976.

Hechinger, Fred M. *Fateful Choices: Healthy Youth for the Twenty-first Century.* New York: Hill and Wang, A Division of Farrar, Straus, and Giroux, 1992.

Hellwig, Basia. "How Working Women Have Changed America." *Working Woman,* Nov. 1986.

Holland, John L. *Making Vocational Choices.* Englewood Cliffs, N.J.: Prentice-Hall, 1973.

————. *The Self Directed Search.* Odessa, Tex.: Psychological Assessment Resource, 1990.

Hopke, William E., ed. *The Encyclopedia of Careers and Vocational Guidance.* Chicago: J. G. Ferguson Publishing Company, 1987.

Hudson Institute, Inc. Herman Kahn Center. *Workforce 2000.* Indianapolis: Author, 1987.

Hummel, Dean, and Carl McDaniels. *How to Help Your Child Find a Career.* Washington, D.C.: Acropolis Books, 1979.

Johnson, Eric W. *Raising Children to Achieve.* New York: Walker and Company, 1984.

Kaufman, Ann. *Are These Things Happening in Your Life Right Now?* Longmont, Colo.: Learnings Unlimited, 1982.

Keirsey, David, and Marilyn Bates. *Please Understand Me.* Del Mar, Calif.: Prometheus Nemesis Book Company, 1984.

Landreth, Gary. "Rules of Thumb for Rearing Responsible Children." Paper presented at the Winter Workshop of the Christian Preschool Association, Prairie Village, Kans., Jan. 1987.

Larson, Bruce. *Believe and Belong*. Old Tappan, N.J.: Fleming H. Revell Company, 1982.

Larson, Jim. *Growing a Healthy Family*. Minneapolis: Augsburg Publishing House, 1986.

Lawrence, Gordon. *People Types and Tiger Stripes: A Practical Guide to Learning Styles*. Gainesville, Fla.: Center for Applications of Psychological Type, 1979.

Leslie, Robert C. *Jesus and Logotherapy*. Nashville: Abingdon Press, 1965.

Levinson, Daniel J., et al. *The Seasons of a Man's Life*. New York: Alfred A. Knopf, 1978.

Lewis, Roy. *Choosing Your Career, Finding Your Vocation*. New York: Paulist Press, 1989.

Malnig, Lawrence R. *What Can I Do with a Major In . . .* Ridgefield, N.J.: Abbott Press, 1984.

McDaniels, Carl. *The Changing Workplace: Career Counseling Strategies for the 1990's and Beyond*. San Francisco: Bass Publishers, 1989.

McGinnis, Kathleen, and James McGinnis. *Parenting for Peace and Justice*. Maryknoll, N.Y.: Orbis Books, 1981.

McManus, Michael J. *Marriage Savers*. Grand Rapids, Mich.: Zondervan Publishing House, 1993.

Michelozzi, Betty Neville. *Coming Alive from Nine to Five*. Mountain View, Calif.: Mayfield Publishing Company, 1980.

Miller, Gordon Porter, with Bob Oskam. *Teaching Your Child to Make Decisions*. New York: Harper and Row, 1984.

Myers, Isabel Briggs, and Peter B. Myers. *Gifts Differing*. Palo Alto, Calif.: Consulting Psychologists Press, Inc., 1980.

"Myths about College Costs." *Kansas City Star,* May 22, 1988.

Newman, Barbara M., and Philip R. Newman. *Development through Life: A Psychosocial Approach*. Homewood, Ill.: The Dorsey Press, 1979.

Olson, Richard P. *A Job or a Vocation?* Nashville: Thomas Nelson, Inc., 1973.

Otto, Luther B. *How to Help Your Child Choose a Career*. New York: M. Evans and Company, 1984.

Overholt, William A. *Choosing a Life-Work in a Changing World*. Mimeographed booklet.

Page, Bill. "The Difference That Play Makes." Mimeograph sheet, Peterborough, N.H.

Paradis, Adrian. *Planning Your Career of Tomorrow.* Lincolnwood, Ill.: VGM Career Horizons, Division of National Textbook Company, 1986.

Rogers, Fred, and Barry Head. *Mister Rogers Talks with Parents.* New York: Berkley Books, 1983.

Schramm, Mary R. *Gifts of Grace.* Minneapolis: Augsburg, 1982.

Schulberg, Budd. "My Wonderful Lousy Poem." *Family Weekly,* October 11, 1964.

Sher, Barbara. *Wishcraft: How to Get What You Really Want.* New York: Ballantine Books, 1979.

Snelling, Robert O., Sr., and Anne M. *Jobs! What They Are . . . Where They Are . . . What They Pay.* New York: Simon and Schuster, 1989.

Stinnett, Nick, and John DeFrain. *Secrets of Strong Families.* New York: Berkley Books, 1985.

Strong, Edward K., Jr. *Strong-Campbell Vocational Preference Test.* Stanford: Stanford University Press, 1985.

Super, Donald E. *The Psychology of Careers: An Introduction to Vocational Development.* New York: Harper and Brothers, 1957.

Super, Donald E., Reuben Starishevsky, Norman Matlin, and Jean Pierre Jordan. *Career Development: Self-Concept Theory.* New York: College Entrance Examination Board, 1963.

Trueblood, Elton. *Your Other Vocation.* New York: Harper and Brothers, 1952.

―――. *The Common Ventures of Life.* New York: Harper and Brothers, 1949.

U.S. Department of Labor, Bureau of Labor Statistics. *Employment Projections for 1995,* March 1984.

―――. *Occupational Outlook Handbook.* Bulletin 2300. April 1994.

Whitehead, Evelyn Eaton, and James D. Whitehead. *Seasons of Strength: New Visions of Adult Christian Maturing.* New York: Doubleday, 1984.

Williams, Dorothy, and Lyle Williams. *Helping Your Teenager Succeed in School.* Loveland, Colo.: Family Tree Group, 1989.